Cal

Hope all is

with you and your

loved ones.

Life is Good dear

Brother, and I trust

that you can with

Great Hope in Christ

Continue to serve and

Care for your people

B. J. Weber

UNCOMMON
PRAYER

UNCOMMON PRAYER

APPROACHING INTIMACY WITH GOD

Kenneth Swanson

A BALLANTINE/EPIPHANY BOOK
BALLANTINE · NEW YORK

A Ballantine/Epiphany Book
Copyright © 1987 by Kenneth Swanson

Grateful acknowledgment is made to the following for per-
mission to reprint previously published material:
National Council of the Churches of Christ in the U.S.A.:
Scripture quotations from the Revised Standard Version of
the Bible. Copyright 1946, 1952, 1971 by the Division of
Christian Education of the National Council of the
Churches of Christ in the U.S.A. Used by permission.
    Strong Arm Music: excerpt from the lyrics to "Mercedes
Benz" by Janis Joplin. © 1970 by Strong Arm Music. All
rights reserved.

Library of Congress Cataloging-in-Publication Data

Swanson, Kenneth, 1948–
    Uncommon prayer.

    "A Ballantine/Epiphany book."
    1. Prayer.   2. Spiritual life—Anglican authors.
I. Title.
BV215.S84   1987   248.3   87-47502
ISBN 0-345-33783-2

Design by Holly Johnson
Manufactured in the United States of America

First Edition: September 1987
10 9 8 7 6 5 4 3 2 1

To Barbara

CONTENTS

GOD DOESN'T HAVE FAVORITES,
BUT HE DOES HAVE INTIMATES.

UNCOMMON PRAYER

DISCOVERING PRAYER

MY CLOSEST FRIEND in recent years has been a man named B. J. Weber. We first met in New York City, where I was on the staff of St. Bartholomew's Church, set amidst the gleaming corporate towers of Park Avenue, and he was running a street ministry in Times Square. B.J. is big and burly, a rugby player. I was attracted by his fierce devotion to God coupled with an ability to laugh easily at himself. Early in our friendship we committed ourselves to meeting for a couple of hours each week to share concerns, talk theology, and pray. B.J. had a rather colorful past. Ten years before, in the midst of a wildly nihilistic, self-destructive spree in Iowa, he had stopped at New Melleray Abbey in order to buy a few loaves of the monks' bread. He remained there for seven years.

During those years, B.J. was often under the spiritual direction of a monk named William Wilson. He spoke so often of what Father William had said about a variety of spiritual subjects that for me this Trappist monk began to assume the spiritual authority of people like Anthony of Egypt, Francis of Assisi, and John Wesley. In December of 1981 B.J. told me that Father William was coming to New York. I faced a swirl of

3

emotionally charged questions. Would he really prove to be so saintly? What did I need to ask him? Would he like me?

We were to meet late on a Friday afternoon in B.J.'s office, at the Lamb's Manhattan Church of the Nazarene on Forty-fourth Street, just east of Times Square. It was early December, already dark as I trudged across town. A raw, sleety, wind-whipped rain biting into my hands and face made me progressively crabbier. When I finally arrived, I was utterly surprised by the man I encountered. William Wilson had close-cropped gray hair and beard, and although he was of average size, he was so unassuming, so unobtrusive, he seemed to recede into himself. He was the kind of person I generally ignored, simply because I would never even bother to take notice. I was disappointed and irritated.

Of course, he hadn't let me down. My own expectations had. In America we equate greatness with force of personality. The great are seen as larger than life; Father William appeared smaller. He once began a conference on prayer by saying to those eagerly gathered, "I don't know anything about God. I know very little about prayer. I hardly know anything about myself." It took over an hour of conversation before I began to tune in to him. He had no agenda. He didn't try to impress or convince. He accepted me as his equal, without any pretense or guile. I had never talked to an adult like him before.

After a time we began to hear shouts and the sound of breaking glass coming from Forty-fourth Street, where young people were beginning to line up at the Savoy Theatre for a rock concert. Looking out the window, I saw several dozen teenagers milling, drinking beer, and smoking dope as they waited to be first inside. When, half an hour later, we heard shouts and screams, all three of us rushed to the window. The crowd had swelled to a few hundred, and fights had broken out, causing large groups to spill into the street. The roiling crowd, out in the rain, took on a sinister, hellish quality. They seemed so mindless, so bent on consuming themselves. Father William had his hand on my shoulder, giving himself better leverage to look out the window. We stood for a moment in disturbed silence before he said, "The only difference between them and us is that we pray."

Pray? Some people do, but most don't, except when they're in the midst of a crisis. Many people who do pray just go through the motions, never expecting God to answer. Yet every Christian, if not every person, has some thoughts about God. Everyone has a personal theology. Even if it is primarily unconscious and seldom articulated, every person thinks about God in a particular way: he exists; he doesn't exist; he cares about me; he couldn't care less about me; he wants me to think and act in a certain way; he doesn't care what I think or do, or if he does, I'll deal with it later; prayer and worship are crucial to my well-being; I only pray when all else has failed; God doesn't hear or answer prayer, so why bother?

Consequently prayer and theology are very closely related. What we think about God shapes the way we experience him in prayer, and how we experience him in prayer transforms what and how we think about him. A liberal Protestant whose theology reduces

Christianity to the rationalistically benevolent "fatherhood of God and brotherhood of man" could not comprehend a "born-again" experience with the risen Lord Jesus Christ. Something would have to give. Perhaps he would be forced to change the way he perceived God, or perhaps his rationalism would be so dominant that he would try to deny his experience, or recast his experience in a way agreeable to his theology. On the other hand, a Fundamentalist Christian who equates God's love with success and material blessing would have her theology badly shaken by bankruptcy, divorce, debilitating illness, or other personal catastrophe. Again, something would have to give. Perhaps her suffering would become the platform for entry into the passion of Christ, or she might redouble her efforts to achieve new blessings as a sign of God's love, or she might stop believing altogether.

I believe that religious truth is best expressed through narrative. My own story illustrates how personal theology and prayer are linked together. I spent over half my life without prayer. But for the past fifteen years prayer has been the heart of my being, and it has unexpectedly transformed what I think about God.

YEARS BEFORE FAITH

I descend from a line of clerics. My maternal grandfather, James McKendry, was a Baptist minister, as was his brother Clarke; my maternal uncle, Merton McKendry, is a Presbyterian minister; and my father, Neil, is a Congregational minister. Church was simply woven into the fabric of my childhood, first in suburban Minneapolis, then in suburban Milwaukee, and finally in suburban Toledo. Although church, with Sunday school, vacation camps, and youth groups, was prominent in my life, personal faith was not. The dominant feeling I had about things Christian was mild resentment, because as the "preacher's kid," I was expected to be a model of decorum. Even so, I did share the sentiments of many other nominal Christians, feeling a nice glow during candle-lit Christmas Eve services, and being stirred to a patriotic religiosity by a packed church thundering out "Onward Christian Soldiers."

One early spiritual memory was rooted to a series of stories published in the magazine *Boys' Life*, about a small group of boys who built a time machine. In it they traveled to Sparta in ancient Greece, and to some fantastic city far off in the future. This captured my imagination. Before I fell asleep at night, I would sometimes be swept along in a reverie of time travel. I knew exactly where I wanted to go: to travel back in time, back to ancient Palestine, so that I could see the face of Jesus. I longed to see Jesus, to know what he looked like.

As I grew older, God simply remained a vague notion. He had nothing to do with the way I lived my life. I never prayed, about anything. My primary goal was to win and hold the approval of my peers. The only moral constraint I felt was fear, of the contempt of my friends, and of the power of my parents and other authorities to punish me. At fourteen, I was devastatingly humiliated when I was arrested for shoplifting in Gimbel's Department Store. Until that time I had stolen often, usually shoplifting, without feeling much remorse.

Other issues also led to anxiety. I responded to a rampaging sexuality by going as far as the feminine objects of my advances would let me. Some offered no resistance. I started smoking when I was thirteen, a fact that had to be hidden from both parents and coaches. The result of all this was the secret life most adolescents have to cope with, along with the guilt dammed up in the subconscious, exuding a constant unease, and occasionally slopping over to cause real pain.

My father seemed perfect, never raising his voice or losing his temper, in spite of often being visibly angry. Since he was a minister, and spoke so easily about God, I assumed God was like him. Once, after I'd been caught drinking, he asked me why I'd done it. I whined something about all the other kids doing it. "Never let me hear you say that again," he snapped with icy fury. "That's the excuse of a weakling." It was the last time I consciously revealed any weakness to him.

In 1966 I decided to attend the University of Wisconsin in Madison, so I could be with friends from Milwaukee. Free from the constraints of my parents, I began to fill my natural contours. I joined the Delta Upsilon fraternity, after being told during rush that a D.U.'s idea of a good time was to sit around the house in his underwear and drink beer until he puked. Besides, all my buddies from Wauwatosa East High School, where I'd gone for two years, were D.U.s. I majored in sloth. After my first semester as a freshman, I never registered for a course that met before

11:00 A.M. I frequently slept twelve hours a night, and spent hours every day playing sheepshead, the local gambling card game, and drinking beer.

It was very difficult to remain uninvolved and self-absorbed in Madison during those years. The campus was so highly politicized, students were forced to take sides on such issues as the Vietnam War, minority rights, and local labor disputes. Demonstrations and even rioting became commonplace. The gross brutality of the sheriff's deputies called in to control demonstrations quickly radicalized me. Over those few years, I was involved in so much rioting, I unwittingly became an expert at managing unruly, panicky crowds during street demonstrations.

I began to casually use hallucinogenic drugs, marijuana and hashish, but after a time, LSD, peyote, and opium. In the beginning I took drugs simply for pleasure. But as I found myself probing psychic, or supernatural, levels of consciousness, I became aware for the first time of experiencing a nonmaterial reality. Without understanding what it entailed, I agreed to be led through what Timothy Leary called the "psychedelic experience." I took a very heavy dose of LSD, and as I let the drug carry me off, a friend read aloud from the Tibetan Book of the Dead. These were the texts chanted over the newly dead by Tantric Buddhist monks, in order to guide souls to their final destination. I remember seeing vortices of human spirits being drawn upward, much like some of the images in William Blake's paintings. Soon I was aware of my own consciousness leaving my body and circling around the room before plunging into an uncharted darkness. I was traveling at great speed. Ahead pinpoints of light shone in the dark. As I approached these lights, I could see they were connected in patterns, almost like molecules. But I sped beyond them into further darkness, before new lights, like stars, began to appear all around me. Traveling at even greater speed, I knew that I was heading toward a particular cluster of lights, and then that I was being drawn toward a single starry light. At incredible speed, I realized I was going to enter that light and, in the same moment, that *the light was God!* Finally, in the instant before smashing into it, I was convinced *I was the light! God and I were the same! I was God!* Then, *boom!* Ken Swanson was utterly obliterated. It took me days to reintegrate.

Although I was badly shaken, there was no denying that my life had been turned on its head. I became consumed with the desire to recapture that experience, and make it a permanent possession. I regularly dropped acid, not for sensual pleasure, but as the vehicle for this spiritual quest. Using LSD to blast off, I discovered I could explore psychic space. The LSD was always very powerful and sent my consciousness on a designated trip, out and back, without any side trips. Yet I soon discovered that if I smoked marijuana and hashish while on a trip, they could be used like booster rockets, sending me off in odd directions, before returning to the course determined by the LSD. After a few trips, I realized that I could get off the designated trip myself, move off in a lateral direction, and then move off that plane in an entirely new direction, and so on. Usually, I was able to make these explorations, and at the same time maintain contact with material reality. However, I sometimes got lost, and was badly frightened, before realizing that the acid would eventually reassert itself, draw me back to the designated course, and, ultimately, as the chemical used itself up, bring me back to a normal consciousness.

Soon I knew enough to get off on short trips by simply smoking marijuana, and only used LSD for special expeditions. The more time I spent out there, the more familiar I became with the terrain. I saw that there were distinct levels of consciousness, and as I learned how to recognize the second level, then the third level, my desire was to go higher, to the place where I knew I would again encounter God, and experience the unity between God and all things. What I wanted to own was the reality that I was God.

These early explorations were usually made alone, but at times a friend might come with me part of the way. The space I explored was always empty, at first. After a time I began to enter zones with shadowy landscapes and buildings. Sometimes I would be confronted by beings, mostly with human features, but occasionally they were monstrous. These incidents left me petrified with fear. Even though I could assure myself, once I was back, that they were simply projections of my own psyche and imagination, I never lost an unsettling sense that these beings and places had an objective reality of their own.

Once I was tripping with three friends, and after I had peaked, and was on the return, I suddenly found myself dropped out of the trip, into normal consciousness. When I shared this with my friends, one of them rolled a huge, fat marijuana cigar. On lighting it, he said we should pretend that each puff would be the last hit we would ever get, so make it count. I did, and in an instant was back on my trip. After a time, I looked down at my hands and noticed that the cigar, which I was still holding, had burned right through my fingers. I had felt no pain, and my instinctive reaction was that I was dead.

The horror of that realization flung me far off into space, to a dark, cramped place I had never been before. It was as if I had been locked inside a coffin. There was a horrible, monotonous creaking noise that never let up. I could see the real world, shining like a jewel, far, far off in the distance, but felt I would never be there again. I was dead, and condemned to hell, where I would remain forever. The dread and terror and pain that racked me were unbearable. After what seemed like an eternity, my friends found me, and during hours of caring talk, led me back.

My psychic well-being had been shattered. It took days before I could distinguish between normal and supernatural realities. I was psychically wounded, and the only reason I didn't have to be hospitalized was because my friends took care of me. They assured me that this was part of my spiritual quest, and that I would come through it with tremendous power. In spite of their concern, I had never felt so alone. No one could understand what had happened and was continuing to happen to me. During this time, I experienced why marijuana and LSD are called hallucinogens. At night, when I would lie in bed hoping to sleep, pinpoints of colored light would appear on the horizon of my consciousness. Flashing toward me, they would contort into hideous, demonic faces, cruelly laughing or malevolently screaming, as they rushed right through my being.

In my agony, I cried out for help, even though I didn't expect any. Once I saw my father's face, and I clung to it, but it did no good. Then one night, when I felt I could bear it no longer, I saw the shadowy figure of a man standing at the foot of my bed. He had long hair and a beard, and looked very strong. He just stood there, in a kind of white robe or tunic, with his arms folded across his chest. His eyes held mine in a steady gaze, and an ironic smile played about his lips, as if he were saying to me, if you only knew how pitiful and weak and stupid you really are. I slept very deeply that night, and although I only infrequently caught sight of him after that, I always had the sense that he was nearby if I needed him.

After a time, I set out again on my spiritual journey, no longer with eager confidence, but with a grim inevitability. Although I was still wounded, and could feel that the terror out there was stalking me, I knew too much to go back. In my own mind, this was a holy quest. I had experienced the reality of God, the reality that I was God, and I wanted to possess it. I was wiser, and warier. I knew the danger of LSD, and from that time used it only with the greatest care, since I really didn't need it anymore for my searching.

But I also discovered that I had become psychologically addicted to marijuana. I had to be high all the time or I couldn't bear my existence. Recognizing that I needed guidance, I sought out people reputed to be spiritually advanced, but the ones in Madison always disappointed me. I felt that I already knew more than they did, and many of them were into weird power games. Instead, I turned to literature, devouring books on the occult, and carefully studied Hindu and Buddhist texts. Soon I was experimenting with yogic techniques. Much of what I read covered ground I had already experienced while using drugs, yet it provided a theoretical framework that was helpful. A great deal of my reading enabled me to carefully probe new areas. I was only mildly interested in how much of this literature was preoccupied with psychic power. Everything I read about I would experience, such as precognition, telepathy, and the "buzz of life," but those things had little allure. I cared only about what would enable me to climb higher and higher through different levels, while still allowing me to remain connected to the first level of consciousness. My great fear, the one that never left me, was to again be cut off from the material plane, with no way back and no protection against the terror.

In the winter of 1969–70, certain events took place that further jarred my spiritual sensibilities. One afternoon, instead of going to class, I decided to read from the Bible in order to begin "rounding out" my spirituality. I smoked some powerful dope that smacked me way out, and drank about a pint of whiskey to keep myself tethered, and began to read the Sermon on the Mount. The content had little effect on me, but while reading it I felt as if there were a breeze, a cooling, fresh breeze, blowing out from the pages of the Gospel of Matthew, clearing all the pollution in my head.

At Christmastime that year I had become engaged to Barbara Burden, whose family lived next door to my parents on Maui in Hawaii. Barbara also attended the University of Wisconsin. Although we had dated for a long time, she never became involved in drugs or in exploring the occult. We were home for the holidays, and I went to a Christmas Eve service with her at Good Shepherd Episcopal Church in Wailuku. When we sat down in the pew, she knelt to pray. I found myself cut off, and very agitated. Who was she praying to anyway? I believed that God was an impersonal force or consciousness, and that everything, including me, was God. But I could sense that her prayer had little to do with all that.

The spring semester of 1970 was chaotic and violent. A bitter teaching assistants' strike shut down the campus for several weeks, and immediately after it had been settled and classes resumed, American troops invaded Cambodia. Campuses all across America exploded in angry protests, and the rage of students was further fueled by the murder of young people at Kent State University. A revolutionary fervor gripped Madison. The National Guard was called in, and armed troops with tanks and other armored vehicles patroled the streets. It was hard to believe we were in America. In the midst of all this intensity, a strange and unexpected factor was thrown in: Jesus people. One assumed they could be trusted; after all, they looked like hippies. But instead of talking about peace and drugs and spacing out, they preached incessantly about Jesus, the Holy Spirit, and the coming of the end!

One of my friends had gone to California to score some drugs, or so we thought. He came back a Jesus freak. This young man and I had once gone on a profound LSD trip together, meeting in an idyllic place to discuss the future. Jesus had never been mentioned. But Jesus was all he could talk about now. I remember one long conversation we had, walking across campus in the spring, when he was trying to convince me to repent. There wasn't much time. My salvation was at stake, because Jesus was coming soon, probably in the next few weeks.

After that I did my best to avoid him. But once we bumped into each other right on State Street. He was surrounded by a group of admirers. He was short, with white-blond hair, beard, and mustache, and had piercing pale blue eyes. He couldn't stop laughing, and said he was drunk with the Spirit. I laughed, too. It was obvious he was high on something, but whatever it was, I wasn't interested. He insisted on giving me a Bible. I took it, reluctant but relieved, since it provided a natural way to break off the conversation. As I walked away, he said I should start with the Gospel of John, and read straight through the New Testament. That made me mad. Who did he think he was? After all, I was the one whose father was a minister.

Two important events happened that summer. First, I was drafted. Since I had registered for the draft as a conscientious objector, I had little difficulty in being granted CO status. I was assigned to work as a janitor at Madison General Hospital. There were about seventy other COs assigned at that one hospital, mostly as orderlies and janitors. I resented the fact that I had been drafted at all, and loathed working at the hospital. Most of my immediate coworkers felt the same way.

In August, Barbara and I were married on Maui, at

Barbara's parents' house on the beach. For me the entire day was spiritually charged. I spent the morning in meditation, and during the ceremony I felt as if we were swept right up into heaven. Our honeymoon on the Big Island was the first period I had spent drug-free in years. When we returned to our house in the countryside south of Madison, Barbara entered graduate school, and I went back to my mop.

I was still staying high, but devoting more and more time to learning yogic techniques. Along with the Eastern literature that was my staple, I slowly read through the New Testament. It became apparent to me that the quality of the spirituality of the Bible was entirely different from that of the occult and Eastern religions. At the time, I couldn't articulate the difference, but I could sense it.

Since I was well connected in the local drug scene, I supplied several of my fellow workers with marijuana. I didn't make much money, but dealing drugs kept me supplied at no cost. One night, in the fall of 1970, I was asked to go to a party at the mobile home of three young men who worked at the hospital. It was a strange scene, rock music blaring, and about thirty people had crammed themselves into the trailer. Barbara was the only woman, and we were the only two white people. To my surprise, I was the guest of honor. Most of the young men lived in Milwaukee and had come to Madison to meet me, because without my knowledge, I was the source of their drugs. I became very high smoking hashish. Every once in a while, I would turn my attention to Barbara, who as usual hadn't used any dope. As she spoke to me, I felt the same breeze flowing from her that I first encountered while reading the Sermon on the Mount.

The following March, a close friend told me about a problem he was having with a mutual friend who wanted to begin a homosexual relationship with him. My close friend didn't want it, but the other man had such a powerful personality, he felt he needed help in coping with the situation. He knew I had been reading the Bible, and he wanted us to trip together and read what the Bible had to say about homosexuality. We hoped to find the answers on our trip.

I didn't want to drop any acid, because much of the LSD in Madison that winter had been cut with strychnine. I'd had a painful, miserable trip on some of it just before Christmas. But he insisted that the acid he had was mellow, and he talked me into taking a quarter of a tab. We went out to our house in the country, and after eating dinner with Barbara, sat down next to each other on our living room couch to begin leafing through the Bible. One of my Bibles had a concordance, so I looked up "homosexual," and we followed the word from passage to passage. I was surprised at the moral clarity of the Bible. The world I'd been living in was basically amoral.

Suddenly, without any indication, I found myself face-to-face with the risen Lord Jesus Christ. He didn't have to tell me who he was, and I didn't need to ask. He said three things to me: "*I am real. The Bible is true. You will never use drugs again.*" I was immediately dropped out of the trip into normal consciousness. My friend sitting next to me, and Barbara in the next room, were unaware of my transformation. Yet in that moment, in the mystery of that encounter between me and God, my life was forever changed.

LIFE AMONG THE BORN AGAIN

I didn't understand what had happened to me. I didn't have an intellectual framework for assimilating what I'd experienced. Yet it came with an implicit moral imperative. That very night, I dragged Barbara and my very reluctant friend all over Madison, looking for the homosexual man. I have no idea what I would have said if we had found him. Probably just that God loved him. I only knew three things: Jesus Christ was real; the Bible was true; and I wasn't to use drugs.

It was far more than just intellectual knowledge. My entire being had been changed. From that moment I had no desire to use any drugs. I discovered that the Bible was a living book. God himself spoke through it. I could learn about him through it, and encounter his living presence in it. And I realized that Jesus Christ was not only real, I could have a continuing relationship with him. How? Through prayer. Not constantly such a vivid, personal encounter as in the moment of my conversion, but a mysterious presence, coming to me at times through my emotions, at times through my intellect, at times through moral imperative, at times through my imagination. Yet at times of his choosing, I would again experience the purity of his personal touch, face-to-face. My childhood wish to see Jesus had been answered. It was an ongoing relationship. He was there whenever I would pray. Those moments of intimacy fueled my desire to know him more deeply.

At first my friends were bemused. They had seen Jesus freaks before. I didn't try to impose anything on them. I even kept a stash of marijuana for guests to smoke. Yet when it was gone, I never bought any more. Gradually I realized that hallucinogenic drugs had nothing to do with a true relationship with God. They were enslaving and led ultimately to spiritual death. Slowly my circle of friends began to shrink. Many of my coworkers at Madison General Hospital became hostile toward me, especially when they realized I would no longer be supplying them with dope. Barbara was happy I wasn't using drugs but remained skeptically detached from this new revelation. I didn't seek out other Christians. I simply assumed that ministers like the ones I knew, and people who attended their churches, would have absolutely no understanding of what I was going through. Most of the Jesus people I knew were so polemical and moralistic, I found being with them unhelpful.

I devoted the next months to trying to figure out what had happened to me. Devouring the Bible, I read it from cover to cover a dozen times in as many months. I was so excited by my new faith that I hardly ever pondered how it related to what I'd experienced in occult and Eastern spirituality. That would come later.

At the time I spent hours every day in prayer, trying to teach myself how to pray. For the first time I became conscious of my own sin, recognizing that I was dominated by such things as selfishness, anger, and lust, which cut off intimacy with God and prevented me from becoming the person God intended me to be. I tried to pray myself free of particular sins, feeling that if I could get to their root, I could simply pull them out. I spent massive amounts of time digging deep holes in my psyche, never getting close to the root of any sin. I knew from my relationship with Jesus that I was forgiven, but I still wanted to become holy in order to please him. After months of frustration and exhaustion, I slowly abandoned the attempt, and moved on to other things.

Many things in the Bible troubled me. I had grown up in a religious environment that reduced the supernatural to what was rationally acceptable. My education had rigorously excluded anything spiritual, and treated religious faith with smug derision. Yet Jesus had told me that the Bible was true. Did that mean that Adam and Eve were actually historical figures? Did that mean that Jonah really survived in the stomach of a big fish? Questions like those dominated me, and I could walk around all day pondering them, as I emptied waste baskets and cleaned hospital floors.

After many months of being alone with my faith, I began to sense two strong imperatives. The first was the realization that it was impossible to be self-absorbed in a relationship with God. I needed to become involved in a ministry, some sort of giving to others. The second was the awareness that I was missing something in my relationship with God. I was alone, and it was his intention that Christians be in fellowship. I heard about a ministry at the Dane County Jail, and arranged to participate. It was there I met Frank Kaczmark. Bearded, dark, heavily muscled, with tattoos all up and down his arms, he looked like a hardly reformed Hell's Angel. I was riveted by his icy blue eyes as he told me with a heavy Brooklyn accent that he had been a heroin addict for eleven years. The only reason he had lived so long with his habit was that he had spent seven of those years in and out of jails and prisons. A little over a year before, he'd had a powerful conversion while in the Alaska State Penitentiary, and upon his release he became involved in ministry to prisoners. He understood and embraced my experience, and became my first spiritual friend.

Frank introduced me to the Madison Prayer and Praise Community. This was a group of brand-new Christians who had spontaneously joined together to worship on Saturday nights. One of the leaders had formerly belonged to the Word of God Community in Ann Arbor, Michigan; others had come from Pentecostal backgrounds. But most were "Jesus people," "Jesus freaks," new, countercultural Christians. The first time I worshiped with them, I knew I was home. These were people who knew the Lord I loved. The worship flowed effortlessly from prayer to song to prayer, mostly praising God. From time to time someone would speak in tongues, or give a prophecy. Usually near the end there would be a spoken meditation on a passage from the Bible, followed by a challenge to commit oneself to God. Barbara enjoyed being there, too, and we soon began making friends.

For the first time I began to be conscious of the relationship between theology and prayer, how what we think about God shapes our experience of God, and how our experience of God changes how we think about him. As I reflected on the Christianity of my childhood, I began to see how the rationalistic bias of liberal Protestantism effectively excludes for most

CLINTON JR. COLLEGE LIBRARY

people any encounter with the living God. This realization made me very angry. I felt I'd been cheated. Others in the community shared my background and anger. Many others in the fellowship had been raised in legalistic and moralistic Roman Catholic or Fundamentalist churches, which had also squelched the living presence of God. They, too, were very angry.

That anger often took the form of self-protective elitism. Those of us who belonged to the Madison Prayer and Praise Community had a vivid sense that we were the only true Christians in Madison. We believed that only people like us truly understood the gospel, and together we had to stand against the apostate church as well as unbelievers. Although my anger was real, this judgmental attitude never rested easily with me. I loved my father, and still wanted his approval. I kept an excellent relationship with Norman Ream, who had been my minister in Wauwatosa when I was a teenager. I was grateful for the help and support many of the campus ministers gave me. But mainly my anger seemed out of place in response to the gracious love and forgiveness I experienced in my relationship with the Lord. As I became more conscious of my own sinfulness, I felt I deserved condemnation. Yet whenever I came before the Lord in prayer, he received me with tender mercy.

However, I tried to become a "true believer," just like the other Jesus people I knew. I carried my Bible around with me as a kind of identification badge. Phrases like "Praise the Lord!" and "I'll pray for you, brother" rolled off my tongue as easily as "Far out!" and "Right on!" had earlier.

When my term of conscientious objection ended

in June of 1972, I had a sense that God was calling me to some sort of ministry. I had been made an elder in the Madison Prayer and Praise Community. After I discussed with the other elders what I felt God's intention for me was, they laid hands on me and commissioned me as a teacher and evangelist. I continued to work in the jail/prison ministry, and added to that the evangelistic work with students and people who had been attracted to Eastern or occult groups.

In terms of practical results, my year as an evangelist was a disaster. As far as I know, not a single person was converted through my ministry. Yet what I learned was invaluable for my future. I realized that even after a year and a half of intense Bible study, I knew very little theology. I could quote Scripture, and had a passionately intense relationship with God, but I had a very brittle intellectual framework for my faith. This became particularly apparent when I would witness to people involved in Eastern cults. I would go into an ashram, and the people would receive me with varying degrees of hostility. I would share with them my experience, and they would simply counter with their experiences. It was at best a subjective standoff. At worst, since I was usually by myself and there were several of them, I would get clobbered. The year confirmed in my own mind that God was calling me to the ministry, and if I was to have any success, I desperately needed a theological education.

The most important theological insight I gained grew out of encounters with devotees of Eastern or occult gurus. I knew that a relationship with God through Jesus Christ felt radically different from an encounter with ultimate reality in Eastern or occult spirituality, but until I was challenged by followers of the occult, and forced to reread Eastern philosophy in order to understand their positions, I had no intellectual structure to support what I knew to be the truth.

In the early 1970s, the most potent Eastern cult was the Divine Light Mission, led by the then "fat fifteen-year-old" guru, Maharaj Ji. In Tantric and bhakti yoga, the key element was the relationship with the guru. It was an ancient practice of Tantric or bhakti gurus to pass the experience of *moksha*, or enlightenment, with a *shakti pat*, a tap on the forehead of a devotee. This meant that the enlightenment which was the goal of all the yogic disciplines, the psychedelic experience of acid spirituality, the ultimate reality that "God and I are one," or "I am God," was available as a gift from the guru. Maharaj Ji was able to dispense this power to many of his devotees, so *shakti pats* from leaders of the Divine Light Mission became the hottest thing going. Whenever I talked to a Divine Light leader, I always found myself locked into an intense spiritual struggle.

One evening I ran into two of them at the student union in Madison. After we identified each other, our encounter became so charged that it was like entering another reality. They smugly insisted that they knew who Jesus was, and I didn't. They were approaching me from a very high level of spirituality. It was as if they were in a beautiful garden, and they beckoned me to join them, saying, "Jesus is here with us. Come in and you will discover him here." They knew that I understood them, that I could look into the garden. The allure was very powerful, and I felt as if I was being drawn in, even against my will. One of the men reached out in order to give me a *shakti pat*, and instinctively I grabbed his wrist and stopped his hand. As I did, the truth rushed into my consciousness with crystalline clarity and beauty. I burst into laughter and said, "Jesus isn't there. You don't know Jesus. I'm the one who knows Jesus!" The vision of the garden shattered and fell around us like broken glass. As they stalked away, I couldn't stop laughing. I finally understood the relationship between occult and biblical spirituality.

Occult and Eastern spirituality is based on a monistic or pantheistic view of reality. This means that there is a direct continuity between all things. One way of understanding this is through an idealistic philosophy. Idealism teaches that behind material reality there are invisible "ideals" that hold disparate things in unity. Take chairs, for example. There are dozens of different kinds of chairs: wood, metal, plastic; some with springs, some with cushions; some soft, others hard; some with legs, others without legs; folding chairs, stacking chairs, beanbag chairs; it goes on and on. What exactly makes a chair a chair? An idealist would say that behind everything we call "chair" is an invisible but very real ideal called "chairness." It is this invisible quality of chairness that makes something a chair. Actually, the invisible chairness is more real than any chair, because chairs are temporal, while chairness is eternal.

The same is true with human beings. Humans come in all sizes, shapes, colors, and temperaments, but there is an invisible reality within each human being that makes us human, and unites all humanity.

In Hinduism this invisible reality is called *Atman*. An idealist would say that this invisible "humanness," or *Atman*, is of far more value than any individual human being, because individual humans are temporal, while humanness is eternal.

Another way of understanding monism is through the insights of modern physics. If one were to take a chair (any chair will do), a book, and me, and were to break down the chair, the book, and me into our invisible yet real atomic structure, no one could tell the difference between the three things. Because at an atomic level there is an essential oneness between everything in the physical universe. It is only as atoms bond together to form molecules that differences begin to appear.

Now a monist, or a practitioner of occult or Eastern spirituality, believes that at the heart of the universe is a basic, primal energy or consciousness which permeates all reality. This primal energy or consciousness emanates and becomes the very stuff of the universe, from basic light and matter to stars, planets, plants, animals, human beings, and according to occultists, other spiritual creatures who populate various levels of consciousness. Although at lower levels the basic energy or consciousness emanates into particular, personal beings, it is itself impersonal, without any descriptive qualities.

This energy is the invisible unity behind all things. It has entered popular culture as "The Force" in the *Star Wars* trilogy. For followers of the occult or Eastern religions it is ultimate reality, their definition of God. In Hinduism it is called *Brahman*, and the goal of life is to experience the reality "*Atman* is *Brahman*,"

27

or "I am God." This experience demands the destruction of any sense of individuality, particularity, or personal uniqueness. Various groups call this experience *moksha, satori, Nirvana,* or enlightenment. It is achieved by passing through higher levels of consciousness (usually seven) through the practice of yogic or shamanistic disciplines, the use of mind-expanding drugs, or the study of esoteric lore. It is what I entered through the psychedelic experience. Followers of Eastern religions or the occult often consider Jesus to be a lower personal manifestation of the cosmic consciousness, as are Krishna and the Buddha, and for them Christ becomes a synonym for *Brahman*.

That is what I finally realized in the encounter with the two devotees of Maharaj Ji. They were equating Jesus with *moksha,* the experience of union with the impersonal energy, or cosmic consciousness, that permeates all of creation. This cosmic consciousness or primal energy truly exists, as do the various levels of the spiritual universe. Even though it obliterates our individuality, we can experience our oneness with that reality. The great mistake, the cosmic error, is to equate that energy or consciousness with God. It is not God. It is part of the Creation, the basic building block of the universe. To call it God, to worship it as God, is, simply, idolatry.

The God revealed in the Bible is holy, existing outside of his Creation. The universe is not an emanation of God's being, but was created by God *ex nihilo,* out of nothing. The God revealed in the Bible is not impersonal energy or consciousness without qualities; he is a living person, or rather three persons living in eternal relationship: Father, Son, and Holy Spirit.

The goal of Christian prayer is to enter into union with Christ, but it is not a unity of being, it is a unity of relationship. We are not God; we are and will always be his creatures. We do not become Christ. Yet through prayer we enter into intimacy with Jesus Christ. Through prayer, through that intimacy, we enter into the life of God. He shares with us his love, his joy, his peace. Jesus sets us free from our sinfulness and selfishness, our obsessions and compulsions, and transforms us into the unique persons God created us to be. He enables us to become people who are free to love others.

Father William Wilson clearly understands this. His abbey, New Melleray, is situated in Iowa near Maharishi International University, founded in the early seventies by the Maharishi Mahesh Yogi of transcendental meditation. In the early seventies, William was living as a hermit at New Melleray. Some leaders from transcendental meditation heard about him and came to visit. During their conversation the followers of the Maharishi insisted that the nonsensical mantras they chanted accomplished the same goal as the Christian "Jesus Prayer." No, no, and again no, William responded. The goal of the T.M. mantras was to empty the mind of all content, all thought, all sensation, all feeling. The goal of the Jesus Prayer couldn't be more opposite. It focused the attention of Christians so that they might be drawn into an intimate personal relationship with the unique, particular presence of the risen Lord Jesus Christ. Of this, William was certain. His entire life of prayer had led him to that certainty.

FROM MEAN STREETS TO NEW MELLERAY

Buddy Wilson, the youngest of eight children, grew up in the forties and early fifties in the Kensington district of Philadelphia. His father was a fall-down drunk who could never hold a job. As a small boy, Buddy remembers bitter, emotionally violent clashes between his parents. Finally his mother threw his father out, and replaced him with a boyfriend. Although shamed by the drunkenness, fights, and poverty of his home, Buddy was still better off than some of his friends. The streets of his neighborhood had their own rules. As a young teenager he joined a gang called the "Hobos." A bodybuilder, he eventually fought his way up to be number two in the gang's hierarchy. The gang's round of activities consisted almost exclusively of brutal violence, forced sex with neighborhood girls, and drunkenness.

He attended Catholic schools run by strict German nuns. They provided a just, orderly, clean world where God was a constant factor. He began to wrestle with guilt—not only guilt over his family's situation, but personal guilt stemming from his own activities. Buddy began to see his street life in direct opposition to the demands of God. He struggled with the "dirty secret" of his sexual activity. He hated the brutal violence of his gang, and often found himself pulling punches in fights. He sensed two worlds, one evil, the other good, and realized that someday he would have to make a choice.

He always had a devout streak. Right after World War II, when he was eight, he received a wonderful new toy as a present. He immediately went to his room and sank to his knees, thanking God for it. From the time he was twelve or thirteen he had a series of transcendent experiences, through seeing a full moon, or the colored sky at sunset, or biting into a sweet grape. In the gang his nickname was "Preacher," because he liked to tell them Bible stories. When he attended high school, he would get up and go to the six-fifteen mass, simply because it made him feel good.

At Northeast Catholic High School he began to make friends from outside the neighborhood, whose values were very different from those of Kensington's streets. He met and dated girls whom he respected and wanted to please. He worked hard, at part-time jobs and at his studies, and was able upon graduation to enroll at the state college in Westchester, Pennsylvania. The Catholic chaplain there, named Bill Faunce, was strong and blunt, with a no-nonsense toughness. Buddy attended his masses at St. Agnes' Church. Once, when Buddy asked about how much it would cost to buy a missal, Father Faunce insisted that he take it as a gift. For Buddy this was a magnificent gesture of generosity, opening up a new world.

In 1956, during the spring of his freshman year, as he waited in St. Agnes' Church to make his confession, Buddy found himself absorbed by the masonry of the stone walls. Suddenly he was overcome by a powerful inarticulate religious emotion. He wanted to become like those stones, dedicated solely to God, existing only for God. He couldn't stop crying. In the confessional, Father Faunce tried to comprehend what Buddy meant when he said, "I want to love God." He gave him a book on the diocesan priesthood. After Buddy had read it, he asked him, "Do you want to be a priest?" Buddy had his doubts. He had little desire to evangelize or catechize. Father Faunce then suggested a monastic vocation, and gave him a book on the early history of New Melleray Abbey, a Cistercian monastery in Iowa. The heroic courage and sanctity of those early pioneers with their absolutes of silence, fasting, and prayer presented Buddy with a godly ideal that demanded everything he had to offer. But thinking about a life without a wife or family led to one question for Father Faunce: "Do you think God will be enough for me?" The gruff priest responded, "If you let him."

Calls were made and interviews were set up for June of that year. At the age of nineteen, Buddy was prepared to say good-bye to his family and friends, perhaps not to see any of them again. His decision was met with disbelief and ridicule. No one was more opposed than his mother, who shouted, screamed, and cried. She signed his release only under duress. William also visited his father, whose scornful response was, "You should join the army."

THE MONASTIC

When Buddy entered the Trappist monastery at New Melleray, Roman Catholic religious life in America was at its peak. Over thirty other young men entered New Melleray that same year. It was also the pinnacle of a particular kind of religiosity, which another Trappist monk, Thomas Merton, criticized as "muscular American voluntarism." It was a cult of suffering, an asceticism that pushed men to and beyond their physical and psychological limits. The concept was that the more it hurt, the more spiritual it was.

At first Buddy embraced the life, and even entered into competition with his brother postulants. He would try every day to be the first at the daily office. When it was time to bale hay or pick potatoes, he would disdain wearing gloves. For him cuts on his hands became signs of his great piety. He said, "The only way they would have gotten me out was in a straight jacket or a coffin."

Yet he soon began to wonder, what was the point? It was an asceticism seemingly without any redemptive element. The monastery had no theology or practice of mysticism, and it allowed no friendship, or awareness of the outside world. Most troubling for him was the climate of repressed sexuality. The "rule of touch," demanding that every physical contact had to be confessed as a sin, was, he felt, symbolic of an obsession with antisexuality that was enslaving rather than liberating. After he had been there for over a year, he was sent to the guest house to fetch something. While there he saw, for the first time in over twelve months, a woman. She was young and had long blond hair. She wasn't particularly attractive, and was heavily clad, but for days after, every cell in his body cried out for the embrace of femininity.

He persevered and passed through his postulancy

and novitiate and took final monastic vows in 1964. It was then he took the name William. The rhythm of Cistercian life, of the daily prayers beginning at three-thirty in the morning, absolute silence, and hard labor on New Melleray's farm, became his own. He began to study theology in preparation for the priesthood. In 1965 he was sent to a daughter house in Ava, Missouri. Struggling to become economically viable, the ethos of that abbey was one of constant work.

During those years William was troubled by the lack of friendship in the monastery. The great founders of the Cistercian Order, Bernard of Clairvaux and Aelred of Rivaulx, had championed the role of friendship in the community. But following the Trappist reforms, this Christian ideal had become lost in their daily life. The vow of silence kept men isolated from one another. William had entered the monastery the same day as another young man, whose name was Edward. Although the two men saw each other several times a day, it was not until two years later, when they both went to visit the dentist, that William found out Edward's last name and where he was from. Living in such close proximity in silence created other difficulties. Patterns of deep negativity could develop toward someone who had body odor, or slammed doors, or clomped his feet, or had an irritating catarrh. Offenses were constantly being given and received with no way to explain, or to forgive, in order to humanize the tensions of daily life.

One great irony of the Trappist discipline in that era was that it tended to exclude intimacy with God for all but a few saints and mystics. There was no structure for developing a deep personal relationship with God. The Trappist ideal was that their highly regulated life of the daily office, austere disciplines, and designated labor constituted an adequate offering to God. Everything in their life stressed conformity to the community way. Any activity not sanctioned by the elders was seen as a manifestation of rebellious pride. Yet mysticism continually sprang up in the cracks.

While at Ava, William discovered books on the mysticism of union with God. He began to practice the Jesus Prayer, and the invocation of the Name, and enter into *hesychasm*, the prayer of the heart. The desire for intimacy with God, to enter into the life of the Trinity, became his passion. He began to thirst for solitude in a place where there was none. He found himself climbing trees and seeking out caves, so he could spend some time alone with God. Once, when the prior of the abbey found William meditating on Holy Scripture, he angrily told him to put the Bible down and do something useful.

In April of 1968 William was ordained to the priesthood and returned to New Melleray. In the wake of the Second Vatican Council, it was a time of tremendous experimentation. All the old disciplines were made voluntary. The new abbot, David Wechter, had previously been William's spiritual director. He gave his monks great liberty, allowing them to work out their own schedules. Life at New Melleray became a kaleidoscope of individual preference. William, still desiring solitude for his life with God, sought the abbot's permission to live as a hermit in a shack in an isolated corner of the monastery grounds. Eventually he developed a pattern of spending a couple of hours each day in labor, usually trimming trees, and devoting the rest of his time to contemplative prayer. He was aware that many of the monks were critical, considering him a loafer and freeloader, and at times he himself felt his life was so fruitless, he was not worth the air he breathed and the food and drink he consumed. Yet whenever he hit a low point, he was affirmed and supported by David Wechter. There are times in every walk of faith when we live not on our own perceptions, but on those of a trusted friend. People began to come to the hermitage for spiritual direction. That was how William met the newly converted B.J. Weber.

In 1974, David Wechter asked William to become chaplain and pastor at the Trappistine Our Lady of the Mississippi Convent, near Dubuque, Iowa. He loved the active life of serving the convent church, studying and teaching the nuns and guests at the convent, and acting as spiritual director for several nuns and laypeople. Yet after three years he again felt the desire for solitude, and returned to his hermitage at New Melleray. David Bach, the new abbot, did not support the hermit life, but respected Williams' call to it. He did, however, forbid William from receiving any visitors. After nine months in the hermitage, David Bach asked him to become novice master at the monastery. Even though it meant moving back into the pattern of community life he had left ten years before in order to embrace a life of solitude, William accepted.

Living among the novices as teacher and director, William slowly became conscious of disturbing patterns of evil in American society, ranging from public funding for abortion to planned unemployment to massive expenditures for arms. Every human being, in some way, was caught up in a vast network of evil social and economic relationships which benefited the few while exploiting the many. And what about the monks themselves? They lived on a vast tract of rich land, in itself a privilege of the wealthy, where others were forbidden to come lest the monks be disturbed. They sold their grain to huge multinational companies that helped the first world dominate the rest. They, too, were among the guilty.

What did their life as cloistered monks have to do with the gospel imperative to love their neighbors? William felt they had to make some response to the world. The majority of monks at New Melleray felt that their life the way it existed was enough of a response. William disagreed. After months of prayer, he resigned as novice master, and in the autumn of 1981 with his abbot's permission he left New Melleray to go on a pilgrimage among the poor. He didn't know what he would discover. But he knew that God was calling him, as a monk dedicated to prayer, to make some sort of practical response to the suffering in the world.

He was in the first stages of this pilgrimage when I met him that cold winter's afternoon in B.J. Weber's office near Times Square. Yet that day he only briefly mentioned why he had left his community. As we talked about his call from God, and his life of prayer, he kept coming back to the Trinity. William insisted, with a gentleness that clothed the strength and passion of his certainty, that the Christian life centered on the Trinity. Prayer, particularly the prayer of the heart, was an entry into the life of God, the life of the Trinity. It is only from entering into the love of Father for Son for Holy Spirit that we as human beings are empowered to fulfill Jesus' command to love.

THE TRINITY IS THE CENTER

Christian prayer leads directly to the mystery of the Trinity, because intimacy with Jesus Christ results in entry into the life of the Trinity. The mystery is that no one while praying experiences three persons. What we experience is a relationship, an intimacy with one person, the person of God. But all three persons of the Trinity are involved in every Christian prayer. The impulse to pray comes from the Holy Spirit. The Son receives our prayers and intercedes on our behalf with the Father. The union of mind and will between the Father, Son, and Holy Spirit is so perfect that we experience them as one. As St. Paul wrote in the eighth chapter of the letter to the Romans:

> In the same way the Spirit comes to the aid of our weakness. We do not even know how we ought to pray, but through our inarticulate groans the Spirit himself is pleading for us, and God who searches our inmost being knows what the Spirit means, because he pleads for God's people in God's own way.

Even as I know I will never fully understand the mystery of the Trinity, I know I enter into the life of the Trinity every time I pray. The problem of the nature of God, and how he is to be approached, was settled for me in the days following that encounter with members of the Divine Light Mission. The knowledge that it is through a relationship with the person Jesus Christ that God may be known has become the foundation of my being. From that sure foundation my life of prayer moves out and back, not only in exploration of different issues, not only in discovering who I am, but primarily in learning to offer myself to God, hoping to become one with the Son, that he might live in me, and I in him.

Of course I have learned many other things about God and the Christian life over the past fifteen years. Most of this knowledge has come through a daily routine of prayer, study, and ministry. But God has also taught me through several personal crises, which stripped away everything but my faith. I have been to the abyss, and more than once plunged into it. In those moments of agony and desperation, in those moments of seeming godforsakenness, I discovered that I was not alone. God himself was with me. Many of those experiences and insights are in the following chapters of this book.

Sometimes I find myself off on little unintentional "trips." Usually it happens in working through a deep emotion, or in a profound intellectual discovery. Whenever this happens, I thank God that he is not "the process," and not "cosmic consciousness," "primal energy," or anything else in creation. I thank God that he is who he is.

Faith itself is a miracle. There are times, often just before I fall asleep at night, when I find myself right at the edge of my consciousness, at the abyss. Looking back, I can see life, my life, shining, pulsing with all its complex permutations, all its pain and pleasure, sorrow and happiness. Yet, looking out, there is nothing. I can see that there is nothing, and I understand why others who have been there say that ultimate reality is nothing. But as I stand there and gaze out into the nothingness, *I believe!* I am filled with a joyous assurance that comes from beyond my being. It is God's gift to me, and to all humanity, in Jesus Christ. Even in the abyss, even in the nothingness, God himself is with us. Even there his Kingdom reigns. Even there we can enter his Kingdom. How? Through prayer.

2

WHAT IS PRAYER?

A FEW YEARS AGO a very close friend was presented with a major career opportunity. At the time he was an assistant treasurer at a huge multinational corporation, and was being considered for the position of senior vice president of finance at an even larger company. Over the years we had taken a deep interest in the developments in each other's lives. As he talked, I could sense his excitement and anxiety, like the nervousness an athlete feels the night before an important game. As was my wont, because of my piety at the time, I said, "I'll pray for you."

I was startled by his response. "No, I don't want you to pray for me." In surprise and discomfort, I reacted, "Okay, then I'll pray you don't get the job." Leaning toward me, he grasped my forearm and said with cold clarity, "Kenny, you don't understand. I don't want you to pray about this at all. This is something I want to do myself."

TO PRAY OR NOT TO PRAY

Why do some people pray and other people not pray? First let's look at some reasons why people don't pray.

The primary reason not to pray has to do with control. There is a strong need inside every human being to be in control. People who have an extreme desire to control their environment try to think through an adequate response to every possible contingency that might arise from any given situation. They want no surprises and are often successful in achieving their goals. People like this are not likely to entrust their well-being to another person, because that means giving up control. Consequently, these people are very unlikely to pray. Genuine prayer flows out of an acknowledgment of inability and finitude. Genuine prayer means giving up control of our destiny to God. My friend with the job opportunity understood this, and was unwilling to take the risk of prayer.

Many other people don't pray because of the way they perceive reality. It has often been written that we live in a "post-Christian," antispiritual, secular age. It is true that materialism and scientism have dominated Western intellectual life since the time of Kant and Hume. Some deny the existence of God and any other spiritual reality. Others simply feel that if such ultimate reality exists, it is impossible for human beings to experience it. For people like that it would be absurd to pray. Often those who so freely reject the notion of a spiritual reality have never spent ten minutes honestly investigating to see if it's real or not. I believe that our culture has moved beyond the influence of such thinking, and we are now entering a "postmaterialist" age. Many leading thinkers, especially in fields like theoretical physics, realize that it is impossible to confine reality to a space/time continuum. Many people, despite their atheistic or rationalistic beliefs, are now recognizing the emptiness and inadequacy of their own lives, and long for a fulfillment, a satisfaction that only God can give.

Another reason why people don't pray is that they believe it is so difficult. They think intimacy with God is reserved for spiritual giants, like John Wesley or Mother Teresa of Calcutta. They think that ordinary people like themselves could never hope to experience the reality of the Kingdom of God.

The truth of the matter is that God calls out to *every human being* through Jesus Christ. Prayer does not demand any particular talent, or special skill. Effective prayer simply demands a desire to know God, the desire to move beyond ourselves into the richness of God's Kingdom. Of course, many people who have this desire don't have the slightest idea how to pray. Prayer is a discipline, but it is a discipline that anyone can learn. The goal of this book is to teach people how to pray with deep satisfaction.

So why do we pray? Why does anyone pray? There are, of course, many reasons. The most frequent is need. For someone of faith, the habitual response to any personal inadequacy is to pray. This kind of prayer almost always begins with the words, "Help me . . ." No situation is too mundane: it can be muttered while struggling to balance a checkbook, breathed upon entering a room full of strangers, murmured on the tennis court.

For many, this kind of prayer is woven into the regular pattern of living or working. This is the prayer that most often escapes the lips of people who seldom pray. It happens when inadequacy has given way to powerlessness, helplessness, or desperation. It may come as the involuntary cry, "O God!" as a car skids out of control. Or it may come out of the agony of having to cope with a business disaster, a shattered relationship, or a terminal illness. It is very often spoken on behalf of another, usually a loved one, yet surprisingly, often for acquaintances, and even strangers who are in trouble.

Once a crisis is over, most people no longer feel a need to pray. In the film *The End,* Burt Reynolds plays a character who has been told he has a terminal illness. Unable to bear the thought of a slow, painful death, he decides to kill himself. Yet whenever he finds himself caught in the middle of a suicide plan, he changes his mind. How he escapes from each suicide plan, once in motion, provides the film's comic momentum. At one point he decides to swim away from the California coast until the shoreline is no longer visible, and then drown himself. Once far offshore, though, he has the usual lack of courage. Swimming furiously back toward the shoreline, with each stroke he sputters the prayer, "God, if you help me get back to shore, I'll give you fifty percent of everything I own. God, if you help me get back to shore, I'll give you fifty percent of everything I own. . . ." Reaching the shore, exhausted, lying facedown on the sand, he pants, "Thanks God. I won't forget that ten percent."

Prayer that comes out of a sense of need is legitimate, but there is a closely related prayer that is not so valid. Instead of beginning with "Help me . . ."

this kind of prayer begins with "Give me . . ." These prayers are satirized by Janis Joplin in her song "Mercedes Benz":

> O Lord, won't you buy me a Mercedes Benz?
> My friends all drive Porches;
> I must make amends.

People who pray this way, and most Christians succumb to it fairly regularly, look upon God as a kind of Santa Claus or fairy godmother in the sky. Young men crossing themselves as they stand at the free throw line, or suburban matrons pleading for a parking space in front of their favorite boutique, are among the most visibly preposterous of this type. More sophisticated are the media mavens who build entire ministries on the promise of fulfillment through this kind of prayer. There is no question that this type of prayer has a very strong allure. Not infrequently I receive phone calls from actresses asking that I pray they get "the part," or from investment bankers asking that I pray they will land "the account." Because my understanding of prayer in recent years has changed, I always decline, but with some discomfort, because I subconsciously realize that I then will not be able to ask them to pray for me when I really want something.

It is safe to say that over 90 percent of all personal prayer falls into the "Help me . . ." or "Give me . . ." categories. The irony is that this is not at all what the Bible, or the great Christian saints, understand as the primary motive for, or function of, prayer. Jesus said, "I have come that they might have life, and have it more abundantly." The abundant life that Jesus is talking about has nothing to do with free throws, parking spaces, or any kind of achievement. It has to do with a quality of living that is found solely in an intimate relationship with God.

The Bible does acknowledge that we live in a material world and need material security, but it sees such things as secondary. Jesus also said, "Seek first the kingdom of God, and all these things will be added unto you." In his book *Mere Christianity*, C.S. Lewis puts it another way. "If you aim for heaven you get the earth thrown in, if you aim at earth you get nothing at all." From a biblical perspective, the motive for prayer is to enter the Kingdom of God, a kingdom that is defined solely in terms of intimacy with God. Human beings were created to live in that intimacy. Why do we pray? Prayer is the doorway to that Kingdom.

THE BIBLICAL BACKGROUND FOR PRAYER

Why do people pray? Out of a sense of need, yes. But this need goes far beyond simply getting help in our troubles, or the satisfaction of our desires. Prayer is the fulfillment of a primal need, the need to be in relationship with God. Human beings were created to be in that relationship, and we are not fully human outside of it. St. Augustine wrote that inside every human being is a God-shaped vacuum. We spend our lives vainly trying to fill that space, cramming it with achievements, with material objects, with sensual pleasures. We are never satisfied, we always want more, because only God can fill the contours of the emptiness inside each of us. This is the consistent teaching of the Bible.

Few people realize that there are two Creation stories in the Bible. The reason is that each story answers a different question. The first Creation story, in Genesis 1:1–2:3, was written in response to the question, "Where do we come from?" The answer is quite simple: God created us and the universe we live in. At each stage of the Creation, God paused and saw that it was good. The pinnacle of Creation came when God said, "Let us make man in our image, after our likeness. . . . So God created man in his own image, in the image of God he created him; male and female he created them." To be in the image of God chiefly means to be a person. As God is personal, as God is a person, human beings in his image are persons.

To be a person consists of two things: to have a unique self-consciousness, and to have the ability to be in relationship with other persons. Our identities as unique, self-conscious persons are shaped by the relationships we have with other people. The primary relationship for each human being was intended to be with God himself, sharing fully in his life and honoring him as Creator. The first Creation story relates that after he created humanity in his image, and knew the blessings human beings would enjoy in relationship with him, God saw that it was very good.

Anyone pondering the first Creation story might well ask, "If God created the universe, and at each stage of Creation saw that it was good, and after the creation of human beings in his image saw that it was very good, *what went wrong?*" The second Creation story, in Genesis 2:4–3:24, answers that question. It is the story of the Fall, the story of how humanity, in Adam and Eve, rejected intimacy with God in order to worship self. It was God's intention for human beings to find their identity not in self, but in their relationship with him. The rejection of that relationship in the Fall represented a collapse on self, which is how I define sin. Lost was intimacy with God, the sharing in his life, the receiving of his love, his joy, his peace.

The consequence of this original sin was three kinds of death: "judicial death," the realization that rejecting the relationship with God meant being cut off from his eternal life; "spiritual death," the awareness of God's wrath, coupled with the realization that human beings can do nothing to restore the lost relationship; and finally, "physical death," which, as James Denney wrote, is simply a negative sacrament, the outward and visible manifestation of an inward, spiritual disgrace.

It is at this point that the real story of the Bible begins, the story of the restoration of humanity to intimacy with God. Though mankind could do nothing to accomplish this restoration, God himself could and did. The story of the Bible can be reduced to a simple sentence: God redeems helpless humanity. God implemented his plan of salvation in human history in a pattern of promise and fulfillment. The initial promise went to Abraham. God singled him out from all humanity and told him that through his descendants, salvation, or restored intimacy with God, would come to the whole world. The promise was refocused during the Exodus, when the nation of Israel entered into a covenant with God. He would be their God, and they would be his people, a kingdom of priests, whose task was to bring salvation to humanity. The promise was redefined through the prophet Nathan, when God declared he would establish forever the throne of a descendant of King David.

From that time Israel looked for the Messiah to be the one who would bring salvation and inaugurate God's Kingdom on earth. The messianic promise was enriched by later prophets, such as Jeremiah and Ezekiel, who saw God's Kingdom in terms of the relationship between God and humanity. On the Day of the Lord, when his Kingdom would be established, God promised,

> I will put my law within them, and I will write it upon their hearts; and I will be their God, and they shall be my people. And no longer shall each man teach his neighbor and each his brother, saying, "Know the Lord," for they shall all know me, from the least of them to the greatest, says the Lord; for I will forgive their iniquity, and I will remember their sins no more. (Jer. 31:33–34)

Alongside these messianic prophecies in the Bible is an entirely different stream of prophecy which revealed God's promise of salvation. These prophecies go under the title of "The Suffering Servant." The prophet Isaiah wrote of one who was

> despised and rejected by men; a man of sorrows and acquainted with grief, . . . Surely he has borne our griefs and carried our sorrows; yet we

esteemed him stricken, smitten by God, and afflicted. But he was wounded for our transgressions, he was bruised for our iniquities, upon him was the chastisement that made us whole, and with his stripes we are healed. All we like sheep have gone astray; we have turned every one to his own way, and the Lord laid on him the iniquity of us all. (Isa. 53:3–6)

Jesus Christ began his public ministry proclaiming that the Kingdom of God was at hand. Through what he said, and far more important, by what he did, Jesus declared that he was the fulfillment of the promise to restore humanity to intimacy with God. He was not just the Messiah, he was Emmanuel, "God with us." He was God the Son, who existed in eternal intimacy with God the Father. He was the Incarnation of God, God come to us as a human being in order to redeem us. He was not just the Messiah, he was the Suffering Servant. As sin, the collapse on self, destroyed humanity's relationship with God and resulted in death, the death of the Suffering Servant as an offering for humanity's sin destroyed the power of sin and death.

God the Father raised Jesus Christ from the dead on Easter, as the fulfillment of the promise first given to Abraham. In his resurrection, Jesus represents humanity restored to intimacy with God the Father. This intimacy is offered to all human beings through a relationship with Jesus Christ. Since he is the one who shares fully in the life of God the Father, by entering into relationship with Jesus, we enter into the life of God. At Pentecost, the risen, ascended Lord sent the third person of the Godhead, the Holy Spirit, to the church to make intimacy between God and humanity a personal reality.

In a relationship with God, he shares his life with us, and slowly transforms us into the human being he intends us to be. As God fills the empty space inside us, we discover not only what it means to be fully human, we discover our own personal identity. In the mind of God, every human being exists in completion. We are not yet that person, the person God intends us to be. We become that person at the Resurrection. Yet when we pray, when we enter into relationship with God and are drawn into his life, we enter into our own resurrection in that moment. The future, our own future in God, breaks into our present reality. The vacuum inside us is filled. We begin to become the people we were created to be.

What does this relationship with God feel like? It is analogous to any other intimate relationship, except that this relationship comes with the overwhelming realization that the person we are in communion with is the Creator and Sustainer of the universe. It brings the awareness that I am all right, that God is for me, cares about me, loves me. In reflecting on the reality of the relationship offered to us in Jesus Christ, biblical writers speak of peace in the sense of well-being, and wholeness. They also speak of freedom, both freedom from our neurotic compulsions and obsessions, and the freedom to make choices that will truly benefit ourselves and others. Just as sin is collapse on self, redemption is a turning away from self, toward God and others.

51

Christianity is about the restored relationship between God and humanity. This relationship exists on several levels, between God and individuals, God and the Church, and God and the entire world. The ability to have this relationship rests entirely on what God has done for humanity in Jesus Christ. The fulfillment of God's promise in the redeeming work of Jesus Christ is an objective reality. It exists in human history independent of any subjective experience of it. We enter into this relationship through baptism and a faith commitment to Jesus. Fostering this relationship, developing intimacy with God, is the task of prayer.

PRAYER AND GRACE

It is essential to remember that prayer, in its widest and deepest sense, is a response to a given, objective status. This given, objective status is the redemption of humanity in Jesus Christ. It is God's intention that people enter this status through an intimate relationship with Jesus Christ. There is nothing we can do to earn this intimacy. It is God's gift to humanity in Jesus Christ, a gift that has already been given. We simply have to receive the gift through prayer. Regardless of what we learn about prayer, regardless of how we discipline ourselves in prayer, any deepening of intimacy with God depends entirely on God's grace and on his initiative. Christian prayer demands discipline, but there is no mechanistic guarantee of mystical insight or dramatic transformation. As Jesus said to the Pharisee Nicodemus in the third chapter of the Gospel of John,

The wind blows where it wills, and you hear the sound of it, but you do not know whence it comes or whither it goes; so it is with everyone who is born of the Spirit.

St. Paul understood that this intimacy with God in Christ was the great mystery of human existence. In his letter to the Colossians he wrote,

the secret hidden for long ages and through many generations, but now disclosed to God's people, to whom it was his will to make it known—to make known how rich and glorious it is among all nations. The secret is this: Christ in you, the hope of glory to come. (Col. 1:26–27)

This mystery was opened to humanity through the cross of Jesus Christ, which was

sheer folly to those on their way to ruin, but to us who are on the way to salvation it is the power of God. (1 Cor. 1:18)

The cross was central because it was there that the power of sin and death were broken. The cross disarmed believers, and opened them to grace. In the thinking of Paul, the Christian life was lived out in that place where the believer's commitment to spiritual discipline was met by the grace of God. As he wrote in his letter to the Philippians,

You must work out your own salvation in fear

and trembling; for it is God who works in you, inspiring both the will and the deed, for his own chosen purpose. (Phil. 2:12)

So the Christian life is lived out in the tension between self-discipline and the free gift of grace. Yet slavishly giving ourselves over to a discipline of prayer doesn't mean we will automatically experience joyous intimacy with God. A discipline of prayer may easily become a routine of life-killing legalism, all form and no substance. When piety becomes rigidly legalistic, many negative things may happen. It is elitist because we begin to feel that only those of us who follow the same discipline, the "right kind of people," are acceptable to God. Piety that has degenerated into law may also be used to manipulate and control others. Yet awareness of the living death of legalism may lead to another error, that of simply relaxing in God's grace and doing nothing. One of the mysterious paradoxes of the Christian life is that it is in the practice of spiritual disciplines that we enter into the grace of God in Jesus Christ. Again I repeat, there is nothing mechanistic about prayer. We can't manipulate or control God with it, but it places us before him so that when he wills, he will come to us.

Any discipline in Christian prayer must be understood in the context of the parable Jesus told about the wise and foolish maidens. Ten maidens went out at night to greet the bridegroom who was coming for the wedding feast. Five of the maidens took care to see they had enough oil to keep their lamps burning through the night, while the other five were careless. When the bridegroom finally arrived, the wise maidens trimmed their lamps and were ready to enter the feast with him. The foolish maidens had run out of oil and were excluded from the feast. The discipline of Christian prayer is simply "trimming our lamps." We can't determine when or how the bridegroom will come, but we can be ready for him when he chooses to arrive. We become like the psalmist who wrote,

> I wait for the Lord; my soul waits for him; in his word is my hope.
> My soul waits for the Lord, more than watchmen for the morning, more than watchmen for the morning.
> O Israel, wait for the Lord, for with the Lord there is mercy; With him there is plenteous redemption, and he shall redeem Israel from all their sins. (Ps. 130:5–8)

UNDERSTANDING THE REALITY OF PRAYER

In spite of the fact that there is nothing mechanistic about Christian prayer, even if it is just "lamp trimming," there is a whole discipline devoted to the theory and practice of prayer. Depending on the perspective of the group practicing it, this discipline can be called ascetical theology, spirituality, spiritual direction, or discipleship. It is a specific body of knowledge that has been developed over the entire course of biblical and church history, designed to foster intimacy between God and a person of faith, through prayer. Prayer is not intended to be a sop to make one feel better, nor is it to be a pious interlude in order to solve problems, or make life a little more pleasant. The goal of a life of prayer is to enable us to become fully human. It is to enable us to enter into the abundance of our own true identity, an identity hidden in God, an identity revealed through prayer.

The reality of prayer is spiritual, and thus invisible. A metaphor that will help reveal this invisible reality is found in the concept of unexplored space. Even though every individual has a unique experience in prayer, the basic territory has been covered by other explorers, and in a sense, their writings are like maps. In *Mere Christianity*, C.S. Lewis wrote that there is a great difference between looking at a map of the seashore, and actually being at the seashore, experiencing it. Almost everyone would place a greater value on actually "being there," but a map becomes invaluable if you want to move from one point to another along the shore, or cross the sea to experience what is on the other side.

Christian writers have been working on maps and anatomies of prayer for twenty centuries. Urban Holmes, Martin Thornton, and other contemporary writers have shaped this information into a very helpful structure. Although every individual's experience of God is unique, there are definite perimeters to the reality of prayer. These boundaries may be mapped out with two crossing axes. The first axis runs vertically between the *intellectual* and the *emotional*, while the second axis stretches horizontally across the first, connecting the *mystical* and the *sensual*. The resulting "Circle of Piety" looks like this:

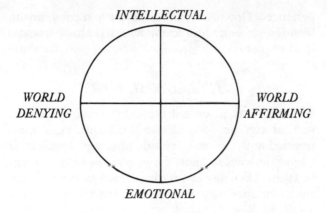

INTELLECTUAL

WORLD
DENYING

WORLD
AFFIRMING

EMOTIONAL

Every Christian is centered somewhere within this circle. Particular personality types tend to occupy a specific area, although most Christians move around the circle at different times. At different times in history each of the four positions has had its champions. In teaching about prayer, I have discovered that it becomes easy to understand the Circle of Piety by simply exploring the lives of great saints who exemplify each of the four particular positions.

One of the easiest ways to learn about prayer is by stretching yourself in an attempt to understand ways of approaching God that seem strange or foreign to you. Consequently these next four sections should be read with great care. As you read, ask yourself which of the four areas best reveals the way you have experienced God. After finishing each section, try to identify someone you know who has that particular kind of piety.

INTELLECTUAL PIETY

Those who tend toward the intellectual end of the vertical axis are not necessarily brilliant, but are interested in the speculative side of things. Intellectual Christians want to know the reason *why* behind issues of faith. Theology is very important to them. They are disciplined and dutiful, and sometimes morally legalistic. They want all aspects of their lives to be clearly defined. They tend to be independent and very difficult to work with in spiritual direction.

Intellectual Christians focus on God as the transcendent Father, awesome Creator, majestic Being, almighty Lawgiver, or even metaphysical Absolute. Jesus Christ is seen as the Divine Redeemer-Revealer, with more stress on his divinity than his humanity. The Holy Spirit is God, of course—the creeds say so—but is not personally relevant for an intellectual Christian. Prayer is reasonable and dutiful, primarily exercised during corporate worship. The sacraments, and great Christian themes like the atonement, grace, and repentance, are facts to be accepted rather than experienced.

This kind of intellectual approach to God traces its roots well back into biblical history. Particularly after the destruction of the temple in Jerusalem in the sixth century B.C., and the dispersion of Israel, Judaism became highly intellectual, a religion of the book. Worship in the synagogue centered around the reading and interpretation of the Bible. The most important religious event in a person's life became a literacy test, the *bar mitzvah*. The most significant religious people in the community were no longer priests who acted out the mystery of God's presence, or prophets who spoke with the living voice of God, but teachers, scribes, and rabbis, who interpreted words written down long before.

During Jesus' lifetime, even though the temple had been rebuilt, the dominant religious figures in Palestine were the scribes and Pharisees, the "doctors of the Law." Faith was measured primarily by adherence to the Law, not only the *Torah* of Moses, but also to the "traditions of the elders," which later developed into the *Mishna* and *Talmud*. Jesus himself was called "rabbi," and was deeply familiar with the Scriptures and the intricacies of the Law. He took obvious delight in intellectually jousting with his opponents.

In the early history of the Church, correct intellectual understanding of both doctrine and morality was extremely important. After the creation of the Church, the Apostles labored to establish the true Christian position against Judaizers on the one hand and Gnostics on the other. Much of their teaching is in the New Testament. As the centuries unfolded, theology continued to be critically significant as Church Fathers like Athanasius (c. 296–373) and Chrysotom (347–407) worked toward a consensus of orthodoxy concerning the nature of God, the nature of salvation, and nature of the Church. The fruit of their efforts may be found in the Nicene Creed. Many thinkers struggled to create intellectual systems that would incorporate all knowledge into the Christian faith. The greatest of these were the systematic theologies of Augustine (354–430) and Thomas Aquinas (c. 1225–1274).

As Europe passed through the fourteenth and fifteenth centuries, many faithful Christians, disgusted by the corruption of the Medieval Church, sought reform. This desire was fueled primarily through an intellectual piety. The Englishman John Wycliffe (c. 1325–1384) and the Bohemian John Hus (c. 1369–1415) called for a return to the teaching of the Bible. Another faithful churchman, Desiderius Erasmus (c. 1469–1536), believed in an intellectual faith. An optimistic humanist, he taught that once people were presented with the "philosophy of Christ," which he called the basic teaching and outlook of Jesus, sound piety and profound charity would flourish everywhere. Behind the work of men like Wycliffe, Hus, and Erasmus was a deep dissatisfaction with the Church, and a great desire to know the redemptive reality of God.

When the Reformation broke over Western Europe in the sixteenth century, its primary power came through the intellectual understanding of men of faith. As a young Augustinian monk, Martin Luther (1483–1546) wrestled fiercely in his spirit with the legalistic demands of late medieval theology. Through the study of Holy Scripture, his despair was transformed into profound joy as he rediscovered the biblical principle of salvation by grace. He rejected the Medieval Church, and built the Reformation on the two intellectual pillars of the sole authority of the Bible, and salvation exclusively through faith in the work of God in Jesus Christ. Later Reformers, particularly John Calvin (1509–1564), created systematic theologies that established Protestantism on a solid intellectual foundation.

As time went on, Europe moved toward an even more intellectual faith. A scientific humanism rooted in the discoveries of men like Copernicus, Kepler, Galileo, Bacon, and Newton, and promoted by the thinking of men like Hobbes, Locke, Leibnitz, and Descartes took root in the European mind. It became clear that knowledge meant power, and many people had the unbounded confidence that human reason could unlock all the secrets of the universe, with the result being a just and happy society. With humanity thus moved to center stage, many of these thinkers believed that there was no need for God, religious faith, or the Church. Various strands of this kind of thinking were woven together in the seventeenth and eighteenth centuries in a movement called the Enlightenment, or the Age of Reason. Some leaders of the Enlightenment, such as Voltaire, believed that Christianity as an embodiment of superstition was impeding human progress, and should be destroyed.

Yet many of the new humanists remained self-consciously Christian, but only at the cost of a complete revolutionizing of religious values. This revolution had to do with authority. For them, the Church, as the bearer of the sacraments, tradition, and historical continuity, was no longer their authority. For them, the Holy Scripture as the living Word of God was no longer their authority. Their responses to God varied from the most stringently intellectual to the most effusively emotional, yet their source of authority became, in the end, themselves. The great issue was, "How do I know that I am saved?" But their answer was found in human reason, human behavior, or human experience. For them humanity had become the measure of all things, even the things of God.

The extremely intellectual aspect of this revolution was epitomized by René Descartes (1596–1650). Born into the French nobility, he supported himself as a soldier and diplomat. But his passion was to discover the basis for certainty in human existence, which he felt could come only through the consistent application of mathematical rules to all questions. His method was to radically doubt all existing ideas. He thus reduced all knowledge to one irreducible intuition, the thinking self. Everything could be doubted, but doubt itself. From that arose his basic affirmation: *Cogito, ergo sum,* "I think; therefore, I am."

Descartes recapitulated all other ideas from this foundation, reasoning that the first distinct idea that the self became aware of was God, whose existence was deduced from the idea of him as all powerful, all wise, and all good. The ability to trust the insights of human reason and the validity of human knowledge rested on the existence of this rational, moral God. Of course this affirmation had little to do with the Christian God. But for the followers of Descartes, the claims of the gospel were sacrificed at the altar of human reason.

The Cartesian methodology depended on a two-tiered view of reality, splitting off the natural (perceived by reason) from the supernatural (perceived only by faith). Later thinkers, such as the Scot David Hume (1711–1776) and the German Immanuel Kant

(1724–1804), insisted on an even more radical separation of reason from any notion of the supernatural. Their principle of autonomous reason left no room for certainty about God. Many began to substitute faith in human reason for faith in God, in the hope that the correct use of reason would result in a just and peaceful world. This fragile hope fueled the scientific rationalism behind the technological revolution of modern society, as well as the call for political revolution by such social critics as Karl Marx and Friedrich Engels.

Yet there were others who insisted on maintaining belief in God, even if it was a faith based on the ethical and philosophical insights of human reason rather than on any notion of revelation. This highly intellectual faith was manifested as Deism among the upper classes in the eighteenth century, and emerged again as Protestant Liberalism in the latter half of the nineteenth century. With knowledge of God restricted to apprehension of a remote and moral "Prime Mover," this approach reduced Christian faith to an affirmation of "the fatherhood of God and brotherhood of man."

What kind of piety could emerge from such faith? Private prayer, and any notion of personal intimacy with God, would be nonsense. Consequently, for them, Christian identity was built around morality, both personal and social. The result was an activistic, work-oriented faith. The Kingdom of God was not to be established by the apocalyptic intervention of God in human history, but by the social reforms instituted by morally enlightened, rationalistic Christians.

The danger of an overly intellectual piety is not just its tendency to make humanity the measure of all things. As indicated earlier, it can also lead to an arid intellectualism and rigid legalism. Yet the history of the Church has abounded in outstanding intellectual Christians, from the great systematizers like St. Paul and St. Thomas Aquinas, to contemporary apologists such as C.S. Lewis and Francis Schaeffer. If your experience of Christian faith was restricted to that practiced at most theological seminaries, you would think that Christianity was almost exclusively intellectual.

I once had a colleague who was highly speculative. Many of his closest friends were theologians, and he constantly read theology. He once spent an evening with a well-known church historian discussing different theories of the atonement. He told me that he was so energized by their conversation that he couldn't fall asleep after returning home. For him as for many others in the history of the Church, intimacy with God was approached primarily through the intellect. What about you? Do you know anyone whose faith is defined by reason or behavior?

EMOTIONAL PIETY

Opposite intellectual types on the vertical axis are emotional Christians. They are interested in experience, not ideas. Often indifferent to theology, they seek out and revel in the experiences of faith, which can be found in charismatic worship, healing ministries, revival meetings, and small "sharing" Bible studies or prayer groups. Formal liturgies and worship services are borne as a necessary burden. The remote transcendence of God the Father removes him from an active role in the life of an emotional Christian. They are, however, deeply attracted to the sacred humanity of Jesus Christ, especially as the suffering and loving Redeemer. The indwelling Holy Spirit, as Comforter and Sanctifier, is also central in their life of prayer. For emotional Christians, repentance and redemption are not abstractions but living realities, and far from being a mere memorial, the Eucharist is a living communion with the present Savior.

An emotional response to the reality of God most certainly has an even longer history than the intellectual approach. Studies in the history of religions and comparative religions have shown that all religious consciousness begins with a sense of the numinous, the holy, the transcendent. The Bible is filled with deeply emotional encounters with God: from the pain of Job to the exhilaration of King David, from the anguish of Jeremiah to the profound contentment of the writer of the Song of Songs, from the marvelous splendor that enraptured Isaiah to the still, small voice that brought Elijah such peaceful certainty.

In the New Testament, encounters with Jesus show a full range of emotional response: the anger of the Pharisees, the shame of Peter, the awesome wonder at his miracles, the joyous table fellowship of his company, the intense gratitude of Zaccheus, the wholesome peace of the healed Gadarene demoniac. The gift of the Holy Spirit at Pentecost transformed the apostolic community from a cowering, defeated band into a powerfully exuberant force that swept away all opposition with a loving assurance.

In the history of the Church patterns of deeply emotional faith emerged during times of missionary outreach and when renewal brought new life to rigid, stultified communities. One such time was in the twelfth century, when the spirituality of the Church had become brittle and dry, and cried out for the renewed activity of the Holy Spirit and the presence of the living Lord. God responded to that cry through the powerful ministry of Bernard of Clairvaux (1090–1153). One of the most accomplished and complex men of the Middle Ages, Bernard became the adviser to kings and popes, and was Europe's greatest champion of the Second Crusade. Of noble birth, he entered the Benedictine monastery at Citeaux in 1112. After three years he was sent to establish a new house at Clairvaux. The reforms he instituted there, which focused on a reestablishment of the virtues of poverty, obedience, and humility, led to a great monastic renewal. During his own lifetime, sixty-eight houses were founded from Clairvaux alone, including the great establishments at Rivaulx in England, and Mellifont in Ireland.

But Bernard's greatest legacy was his sensual or world-affirming, emotional teaching on prayer. In his opposition to the theologian Abelard, he revealed his distrust of intellectual approaches to God. Unexcelled among his contemporaries in his use of language and knowledge of the Bible, Bernard sought always to touch people's hearts rather than their minds. Although he called for total commitment in a discipline of prayer, he was always clear that any deepening of intimacy with the Lord rested entirely on God's grace. Nothing was mechanistic. Believers could only hope to be visited by the living Word of God. For him the key to personal piety was memory and imitation, and the goal of all prayer was to experience the love of God. His primary metaphor for intimacy with God was marriage, which he expounded in eighty-six sermons on the Song of Solomon.

Ironically, the Enlightenment principle of making human beings the measure of reality also manifested itself in highly emotional ways. Such a response of faith came from Blaise Pascal (1623–1662), who remains one of the greatest geniuses in human history. A Frenchman, he was, like so many other Christian leaders, born into the ranks of the lower nobility. By the time he was in his early twenties, he was acknowledged as the leading mathematician and engineer of his day. Extremely modern in his psychological insights, he despised rationalists like Descartes, writing in his book *Pensées*, that they were

> useless and uncertain . . . shallow, game playing, avoided the real issue of humanity's basic forlornness, perilous state, incapacity, discordance, inconsistency, boredom, anxiety, and especially his mortality.

In the midst of a personal crisis in 1654, he sought solace in reading the Gospels. Meditating on St. Peter's thrice-repeated denial of Jesus, Pascal realized his own separation from God, his own desolation, and that in Jesus Christ, he was forgiven. He wrote a journal entry that night, which was discovered sewn into the lining of his coat only after he had died.

> Fire . . . the God of Abraham, Isaac, and Jacob, not the God of the philosophers and schol-

ars. . . . Certainty, Certainty, emotion, joy, peace, the God of Jesus Christ. Thy God shall be my God. Oblivion of the world and of everything except God. Joy, Joy, Joy, tears of Joy!

Pascal rejected reason as a basis for certainty for another kind of knowing, which he called *esprit de finesse*, or "knowledge of the heart." By "heart" he meant the personal, spiritual center of human beings, the starting point of dynamic, intimate relationships. In *Pensées* he wrote,

> The heart has its reasons of which reason knows nothing: we know this in countless ways. . . . It is the heart that experiences God, and not reason. That is what faith is: God felt by the heart, not by reason. . . . Knowing God without knowing our own wretchedness makes for pride. Knowing our own wretchedness without knowing God makes for despair. Knowing Jesus Christ strikes the balance because he shows us both God and our own wretchedness.

In an interesting way, Pascal's understanding of faith took root in the Protestantism of North America. Christianity in the American colonies was dominated by Calvinistic Puritanism, which in stressing the sovereignty of God led to the theology of double predestination. This meant that God foreordained some to salvation and others to damnation. The great question became, "How do I know I am among the saved?" The answer was an *experience* of salvation, usually in response to a call to commitment by an evangelistic or revivalistic preacher.

Revivalism swept the colonies in the First Great Awakening in the 1740s through the preaching of George Whitefield (1714–1770), Jonathan Edwards (1703–1758), and others. After the Revolution, the new nation of the United States was gripped for two generations in the Second Great Awakening, which spread revivalistic fervor westward through tent meetings and circuit riders. Revivalism remained at the heart of American Protestantism through the ministries of Charles Finney (1792–1875), Dwight Moody (1837–1899), Billy Sunday (1862–1935), Billy Graham (1918–), and countless lesser known evangelists, many of whom now present this call to commitment through television.

Strangely enough, Christians who have been drawn to God through revivalism, in America and throughout the world due to missionary outreach, are as much children of the Enlightenment as are rationalistic liberals. For both, they themselves are the final measure of certainty. A revivalist's answer to the question, "How do you know you have been saved?" is not, "Because I have been baptized." It is not, "Because I have put my trust in the biblical claim that Jesus Christ died in my place." It is, "Because I have been *born again!*"

Great revivals and periods of renewal in the Church tend to be marked by emotional spirituality. Charles Finney, the great nineteenth-century American revivalist, had a place set aside near the front of the tent called the "quaking bench," reserved for those about to be born again, who positively shuddered with emotion. Even in our own time at Pentecostal and charismatic worship services it is common to see passionate weeping, exuberant joy, and overwhelming displays of affection, sometimes all in the same person in the period of a single hour.

Needless to say, intellectual and emotional Christians tend to distrust one another. The tension between them can be captured in two stories. One of the great Christians of the first part of the twentieth century was the Dutch theologian and statesman Abraham Kuyper. As a young man he had received the finest education available in Europe. A brilliant student, he completed his academic work with a doctorate in theology. Still in his early twenties, he had become a master of the Liberal Protestant theology which dominated Europe and North America at the time. He was assigned to a parish church in the Dutch countryside. Week after week he preached learned, erudite sermons to his peasant congregation. Week after week the numbers in attendance dwindled. Finally an old, semiliterate peasant woman invited the young scholar to tea. She sat him down in her humble parlor, served him tea and cake, and said, "Dr. Kuyper, I would like to tell you about the gospel of Jesus Christ." Listening to her testimony of a simple, emotional faith, Kuyper was touched by the power of the Holy Spirit and born again into an entirely new quality of existence.

The other side can be seen in a story about another theologian, the late Albert Mollengen of Virginia Seminary. Dr. Mollengen was on a driving trip across the South. Somewhere in Tennessee he stopped for a meal at a diner. As he was in the men's room washing his hands, another man stepped up to wash at the next sink. The other man turned to him and said, "Have you been saved?" Startled, Mollengen turned and responded, "Why, yes." Undaunted, the other pressed him by asking, "When?" With certainty, Dr. Mollengen looked deeply into the man's eyes and replied, "On Good Friday."

SENSUAL PIETY

Do you know anyone who experiences God primarily through his or her senses? A person who finds God in the beauty of the countryside, or in the power of great art or music? Sensual Christians, who make up one end of the horizontal axis, are people who experience God in the world. For them prayer is linked to their senses and is focused on material objects. Yet they are not in any way "worldly." They do not find their security or identity in the possession of things, and may adopt the most severe and ascetic disciplines. They simply discover God in and through the physical world.

Sensual Christians tend to be extremely sacramental, seeing that in every way, grace perfects nature. They fully accept the human body and its senses as a gift of God's grace. Theologically, they champion the doctrines of Creation and the Incarnation, stressing both Jesus' sacred humanity and his role as the cosmic Christ renewing all things. They articulate a love of Creation as the scene of divine activity, experiencing God in the power of a thunderstorm or in the wonder of nature, as well as in the exquisite beauty of a favorite melody or in the smile of a loved one. Understandably, sensual believers will often use icons or other devotional objects to help focus their prayer.

In the biblical understanding of reality, Creation has always been the scene of God's activity. Although marred by the Fall, and thus in need of redemption, Creation itself remained, by God's own pronouncement, good. The care taken with the vestments and instruments used in Jewish worship of *Yahweh* revealed their understanding of the connection between the Creation and the Creator. In the New Testament, the very Incarnation itself was seen as God's great "Yes!" to the created order. Mary Magdalene, and the other two Marys, whose mystical insight was expressed through material things such as precious perfume, human tears and hair, and crumpled grave clothes, were people of deeply sensual faith.

The most powerful infusion of sensual and emotional spirituality came into the Church in the West through Celtic Christianity. Begining in Ireland, Celtic missionary monks settled in Scotland and northern England, before reaching out to evangelize the Germanic tribes of northern Europe. In Celtic worship the cross and the Virgin Mary became objects of devotion, the real presence of Jesus in the bread and wine of the Eucharist was stressed, and Holy Scripture was passionately read and meditated on.

The founder of Celtic Christianity was the British monk St. Patrick (372–466). In Celtic monasticism there were many monks who, in addition to the Office, recited the entire Psalter, all 150 Psalms, every day! Besides the Psalms, many hymns and rhymed prayers were used in corporate and private devotions.

Very common were *lorica* or "breastplate" prayers, used to invoke protection from demonic powers. One such hymn, attributed to St. Patrick himself, is still frequently sung at consecrations, ordinations, baptisms, and weddings. Its first verses read,

I bind unto myself today
The strong Name of the Trinity,
By invocation of the same,
The Three in One, and One in Three.

I bind this day to me forever,
By power of faith, Christ's Incarnation;
His baptism in the Jordan River;
His death on Cross for my salvation;
His bursting from the spiced tomb;
His riding up the heav'nly way;
His coming at the day of doom:
I bind unto myself today.

I bind unto myself the power
Of the great love of cherubim;
The sweet "Well done" in judgement hour;
The service of the seraphim;
Confessor's faith, apostle's word,
The patriarch's prayers, the prophet's scrolls;
All good deeds done unto the Lord,
And purity of virgin souls.

At its best, Celtic spirituality resulted in great devotion to both prayer and ministry, and a transformation of all life into an openness to the Kingdom of God. But at its worst, a morbid fixation on the threat of demons led to the cross and atonement being treated as protecting powers rather than objective realities joyously and confidently integrated into one's life. As if Jesus himself weren't enough, angels and saints were constantly invoked for protection.

Added to this was a focus on sin, which in some ways seemed uninformed of the glorious redemption in Jesus Christ. Uncertainty about forgiveness led to a piety concentrated on penance, with constant petitioning of God for forgiveness. The notion of a Christian "hero," an ascetic champion and warrior of prayer who won salvation through his or her piety, took hold in the medieval imagination. Unfortunately for the laity, to become such a hero, one most certainly had to adopt the life of a monk or nun.

Into that spiritual milieu burst one of the greatest lives of prayer in the history of the Church, that of Francis of Assisi (1181–1226). In the modern world, Francis has often become the object of a sentimentalized romanticism, but nothing could be further from reality. For all his gentleness, he was tough-minded and powerfully ascetic. Although he founded an order of wandering friars, his goal was to make intimacy with the risen Lord Jesus Christ accessible to all people. Devoted to poverty, preaching, penance, and prayer, his piety was concrete, particular, human, and moral. Highly sensual and emotional, he lived in deep communion with the natural order, experiencing the redemptive reality of Jesus Christ in the mundane and ordinary, the sun and moon, animals, birds, and even insects! He developed a life of prayer that concentrated on the imagination, focusing on the Nativity and Passion of Jesus Christ.

Following Francis, popular piety in the twelfth and thirteenth centuries was extremely sensual, concentrating on the humanity of Jesus Christ. Lay societies devoted to such things as the Sacred Heart, the Holy Name, and the Blessed Sacrament flourished. But there was also a continuing loss of clear understanding of the basic elements of the gospel, such as salvation by grace, and the living presence of Jesus Christ in the Church. The belief that salvation must be earned, and that God could only be approached through mediators, remained a persistent problem. Devotion to Mary, and the superstitious veneration of saints, relics, and icons were widespread.

Long after the Reformation, devotion to the Sacred Heart of Jesus received new impetus through the ministry of the Norman priest John Eudes (1601–1680). Eudes taught that the human heart of Jesus was the perfect symbol for the mysteries of Christian faith: Creation, Incarnation, redemption, forgiveness, and loving service for others. The devotion was further spread through the visions received by a French Visitation nun named Margaret Mary Alacoque (1647–1690). She claimed that Jesus himself visited her and instructed her to help spread the flame of his love through his heart which loved the world so much. Chapels and confraternities devoted to the Sacred Heart expanded this devotion through processions and novenas (nine days of prayer dedicated to seeking God's will).

Toward the end of the twentieth century other Christian movements have used sensual piety as the basis for social ministry. Mother Teresa of Calcutta has gained worldwide recognition for her work among the poorest of the poor in India. She and her Sisters of Charity pluck abandoned infants from garbage cans and raise them in an environment of love. They collect dying derelicts from the city's gutters and care for them so they can die with dignity. The foundation of this difficult ministry is a deep life of prayer. When Mother Teresa gets down on her knees and turns over the emaciated and reeking body of a dying man, she says with complete integrity that rather than being revolted, she is filled with joy, because more often than not, she finds herself looking into the face of her Lord Jesus Christ.

MYSTICAL PIETY

At the other extreme on the horizontal axis are mystical Christians. If sensual Christians find intimacy with God through their senses, mystical Christians experience God beyond both their senses and intellect. They grope for a mystical, unmediated relationship with God. Material things are not seen as evil, but simply as a nuisance or hinderance to a pure encounter with God. Their path to God, the *via negativa*, is often expressed in negative terms such as the cloud of unknowing, the dark night of the soul, the desert, or the wilderness. Mystical Christians tend to focus on God the Father as holy, transcendent, and hidden, and often ignore the implications of an incarnational theology. Certain types of meditation and contemplative prayer are extremely mystical.

In ancient Israel many of the prophets had mystical, cosmic visions, such as Ezekiel's chariot of fire, and Isaiah's telling,

> In the year of King Uzziah's death I saw the Lord
> seated on a throne, high and exalted, and the
> skirt of his robe filled the temple. About him
> were attendant seraphim, and each had six
> wings; one pair covered his face and one pair his
> feet, and one pair was spread in flight. They
> were calling ceaselessly to one another, Holy,
> holy, holy is the Lord of Hosts: the whole earth
> is full of his glory. (Isa. 6:1–3)

In the New Testament, Jesus at times allowed his
followers to glimpse another reality, such as at the
Transfiguration when Peter, James, and John saw
Jesus enter a blinding light to converse with the
prophets Moses and Elijah. After Pentecost, Stephen
was enraptured by a vision of Jesus enthroned in
heaven, while he was being martyred. Paul wrote of
several mystical experiences with God he had during
his lifetime.

It was a predominantly mystical piety that took
hold in the Church during its first centuries. This was
partly due to the fact that Christianity took root in the
Greek-speaking Hellenistic culture that was shaped
by a Platonic view of reality. With invisible "ideals"
considered to be of more value than their physical
manifestations, intimacy with God was also sought in
a realm beyond the senses. This view, coupled with
an excessive desire for purity of heart and spiritual
poverty, led many Greek Christians to despise all culture, and often reject marriage, meat, and wine. Self-
castration was not uncommon, and was once celebrated corporately by a group of young men running
through Alexandria's streets holding their testicles

aloft in triumph! The most extreme expression of this type of spirituality was martyrdom, which some Christians openly sought.

The Church faced a great spiritual crisis in the third decade of the fourth century, after the Roman Emperor Constantine became a champion of Christianity. Whereas before Constantine's rule, being Christian had demanded some social, economic, and political sacrifice, afterward being Christian was an advantage. The Church was flooded with tens of thousands who wanted to be baptized for the wrong reasons. Many deeply committed Christians responded to this situation by becoming *anchorites*. The word means "to withdraw," and that they did, to the wilderness or desert, in order to live a life totally dedicated to God, cut off from both the world and what they perceived to be the newly tainted Church. They sought to embody in their lives the Apostle Paul's dictum to "pray without ceasing."

The spirituality developed by these Desert Fathers was extremely mystical. Their strict asceticism of prayer, study, and fasting was maintained throughout their entire lives. Father William told me a story about Abba Poemen, that when he was ninety years old and dying, two of his younger followers decided to carry him on a stretcher into the city, where he could meet his end with greater comfort. On the journey the ancient monk passed in and out of consciousness. As they approached the city, he revived and asked where they were taking him. "Into the city," replied one of the younger monks. "Hmm," he mused. "Are there beautiful women in the city?" "Yes, Abba," was the reply. "Then take me back to the desert."

Although Christian spirituality in Western Europe developed along highly emotional and sensual paths, during the thirteenth and fourteenth centuries, at the height of the Middle Ages, there was a burst of world-denying mystical piety, both in the Rhineland and England. Much of this was fueled by wandering penitential preachers, who called for true repentance and conversion. Many of their listeners responded by joining existing or new monasteries and convents. But many others, particularly those from the lower classes, were determined to live out lives of holiness in the midst of fulfilling their secular responsibilities.

The Beguines were associations of laywomen which sprang up in Holland and northern Germany. Although they took no vows, they embraced a common life of manual labor, chastity, simplicity, liturgical prayer, and works of mercy, based on the Jerusalem Church described in the *Acts of the Apostles*.

The learned Dominican scholar Meister Eckhart (1260–1327) has had wide influence historically as the founder of German mysticism. He wrote that ultimately, God is incomprehensible and can be encountered only in the "darkness of unknowing." Since all Creation is contained in God, there is no other being except God: *esse est Deus*. In relation to his or her being, the creature itself is nothingness, so to encounter God, the believer must leave behind all created things. In his thinking, Eckhart ignored the doctrines of Creation and the Incarnation, and leaped over the biblical categories of sin, redemption, and grace in order to assert the essential unity between God and the individual human spirit. For him, contemplation was the recognition that "my truest I is God." Yet when

he was accused of heresy in 1326, he explained himself by saying,

> It is false to say we are transformed and changed
> into God. Indeed, a holy and virtuous man does
> not become Christ himself nor the only Son, and
> other men are not saved by him; he is not the
> likeness of God, the only begotten Son of God,
> but he is in the likeness of God, a member and
> heir of the true and perfect only Son. We are
> his co-heirs.

Eckhart influenced an entire generation of outstanding Christian leaders on the Continent, including John
Tauler, Henry Suso, and Jan van Ruysbroeck. But an
independent mystical flowering was taking place at
the same time in England. It was a time of tremendous
upheaval, as the Black Death terrorized and deci-
mated the populace. Many believed it to be a sign of
God's wrath and turned to penance and fervent
prayer. With this foundation, the English mystics
tended to be anti-intellectual and contemptuous of abstract thought. Although mystical and world-denying,
medieval English spirituality was always highly emotional. Richard Rolle (c. 1295–1349), a hermit, wrote
that intimacy with the Trinitarian God resulted in a
rapture or ravishing of love he described as fire, song,
and sweetness. The anonymous author of the *Cloud
of Unknowing* (c. 1370) insisted that union with God
could be found only in love, not knowledge. Walter
Hilton (d. 1396), in his treatise *The Scale of Perfection*,
wrote that the essential work of life was a contemplation resulting in "a soft, sweet, burning love" so

powerful "that by an ectasy of love the soul for the time being becomes one with God and is conformed to the image of the Trinity."

More accessible to us as contemporary Christians was the piety of George Fox (1624–1691), an English contemporary of Pascal. He traveled about England and abroad, preaching and organizing the Society of Friends, or Quakers. He believed that anyone could experience an immediate communion with God, and be guided by the "inner light" of the Holy Spirit within the human heart. Thus the Quakers rejected professional ministers, material sacraments, and the letter of Holy Scripture, and sought instead direct illumination by God.

Like each of the other three, an extreme mystical piety leads to an unbalanced spirituality. The ultimate danger of mystical approach is angelism, a dissatisfaction with the human state coupled with a veiled desire to be like an angel. The logic of angelism goes like this: "If God doesn't eat, and I don't eat, I become more like God," or, "If God doesn't have sex, and I don't have sex, I become more like God." Although this quest for a pure spirit by the suppression of bodily senses takes seriously the consequences of human sin as a critical factor in relationship with God, it may lead to a denial of our creatureliness. After all, the Christian hope is in a redeemed Creation, and resurrection of the body.

A BALANCED PIETY

Of course, few Christians are at the extreme ends of any of these axes. It is also important to bear in mind that no one is purely mystical or purely emotional. Each of these four positions makes a claim on an individual believer. But every Christian will fit into one of the quadrants of the Circle of Piety. However, the quadrants are not airtight. For example, someone who is primarily focused in the sensual emotional quadrant, as are most Americans, may very well spill over and occupy space in the other areas. Individuals in one quadrant will often sneer at their opposites, as seen in the long-standing enmity between rationalists and pietists; however, in the context of understanding prayer, absolutely no value is placed on one quadrant over another. As each quadrant reflects a certain personality type, each is equally valid.

Understanding this analysis of piety has value for several reasons. You, too, fit in somewhere within the Circle of Piety. Knowing yourself and how you relate to God can deeply and immediately enrich your life of prayer. And if you desire to grow spiritually, the first step is to learn about other ways of seeking intimacy with God. People with different pieties tend to distrust, if not despise, one another. Historically this has sometimes led to tragic persecution and oppression. In my experience, simply understanding and acknowledging that different ways of approaching God are equally valid for different personality types tends to lead to tolerance and cooperation. It has for me.

Some Christians, of course, have a very balanced piety. Jesus is the primary example of a person whose identity and entire life were shaped by prayer. His piety fills the circle. There were mystical moments, as at his baptism, when the voice of the Father spoke from heaven and the Spirit like a dove descended upon him, or when he was transfigured on the mountaintop. His healing ministry, his use of the mundane in the parables, his washing of the disciples' feet, his institution of the Eucharist in bread and wine all showed his deeply sensual nature. He was intellectual, while still a boy impressing the rabbis in Jerusalem with his knowledge, and jousting with the Pharisees throughout his ministry. His compassion for those who suffered and for sinners, his anger at injustice and hypocrisy, the joy of his fellowship, and the passion of his death all revealed his emotional spirituality.

Although we only know the content of three of his prayers—the Lord's Prayer, his prayer for the Church in John 17, and his agony in the Garden of Gethsemane as he faced death—we are constantly reminded in the Gospels that he went off alone to be in prayer, sometimes for a whole night. Of course, the fullness of his revelation was that he was God the Son. Yet in the Incarnation he maintained his relationship with God the Father through prayer. It was through prayer he manifested an intimacy so profound he could say,

> When a man believes in me, he believes in him who sent me rather than me; seeing me, he sees him who sent me. . . . I do not speak on my own authority, but the Father who sent me has himself commanded me what to say and how to speak. I know that his commands are eternal life. What the Father has said to me, therefore— that is what I speak. . . . In truth, in very truth I tell you, the Son can do nothing by himself;

he does only what he sees the Father doing:
what the Father does, the Son does. For the
Father loves the Son, and shows him all his
works. . . . I and the Father are one. (John
12:45, 49–50, 5:19–20, 10:30)

Other Christians have been able to develop a pro-
foundly balanced spirituality. One such person was
Juliana (d. 1442), perhaps the greatest English mystic.
She lived in a cell which opened into St. Julian's
Church in the city of Norwich. From her cell she could
participate in the liturgy and give spiritual direction
to those who came to her for advice. In 1373, during
a severe illness (perhaps the plague), God gave her a
series of powerful visions, which led to a sober, well-
balanced, and joyously optimistic yet realistic spirituality. Her reflection on these visions was published
in her *Revelations of Divine Love*. Widely read, she
quoted works of the great Cistercians, Victorines, and
Dominicans. Sensual and world-affirming, she centered on Jesus Christ's redemptive presence, teaching
that the sacraments of the church were to be the center
of the Christian life. As with her countrymen, the
meaning of life was summed by a revelation that took
root not in the intellect, but in the emotions.

You would know our Lord's meaning in this
thing? Know it well. Love was his meaning.
Who showed it to you? Love. What did he show
you? Love. Why did he show it? For love. Hold
on to this and you will know and understand love
more and more. But you will not know or learn
anything else—ever!

WHY I PRAY

In thinking about understanding prayer, and the study of ascetical theology, spirituality, and discipleship, I am brought to the realization that I would rather be standing on the beach than simply reading a map of it. I find it helpful to know that my personal piety tends to be mystical and emotional, because it enables me to be more conscious and intelligent about prayer. But I wouldn't trade a single moment of intimacy with God for all the knowledge in an entire library on ascetical theology.

I need to pray, yes, and not just because I so often feel inadequate and am looking for help. I need to pray because I know the emptiness inside of me can only be filled by God. I need to pray because I know that it is only in prayer that I begin to become fully human. I need to pray because I was created to be in relationship with God. I need to pray because in prayer heaven and earth meet, and the reality of God's Kingdom, the future reality of redemption, wholeness, and joyous love, breaks into my present brokenness.

Father William is right. Prayer does make us different. Not better, not even more beloved by God, just different. The difference is measured by a humble desire to proclaim the reality of God's atoning love in Jesus Christ. The difference is measured by a willingness to love, to risk loving people who are desperately in need of redemption.

3

PRAYER IN THE COMMUNITY OF FAITH

AFTER MY CONVERSION in the winter of 1971, I was spiritually a blank slate. I knew just three things: Jesus Christ was alive, and I could have an intimate relationship with him through prayer; the Bible was not just a stale collection of dead religiosity, but a book of life-changing power permeated with the presence of God; and I was suddenly free of any compulsion to use drugs.

But I had no intellectual framework to help me understand what had happened to me. The remote, abstract God of my Liberal Protestant childhood seemed as alien to my new experience as was the occult, Eastern spirituality of my college years. I was isolated. Not only did I not have any vocabulary through which to articulate what I was experiencing, even when I was able to express something, I couldn't find anybody who didn't react to it with discomfort, suspicion, hostility, or amusement.

However, that blank slate began to be written on, in two ways. The first was through prayer. The mystery and wonder of prayer was the reality of Jesus' presence. The more time I spent in prayer, the better I got to know him. What I learned wasn't abstract or intellectual. It was personal, analogous to the knowledge of another in any intimate human relationship. This kind of knowledge was subjective and affective, informing the subconscious and unconscious as much or even more than the conscious mind. Yet through that personal knowledge a structure began to emerge in my intellect. I could use that structure to evaluate the truth of any abstract intellectual statements or propositions about God.

My college roommate was scrupulously, if not punctiliously, honest. He always told me exactly what he felt or thought, even if it hurt or made me angry. Once, when I was involved in a beery late-night card game, somebody mentioned him. Another player said, "That b—— s——!" I jumped all over the guy. Not only was it obvious to me that he didn't know my roommate, he compounded it by totally misrepresenting him. For me the same kind of thing became true about Jesus. I began to test what other people said or wrote about Jesus by what I knew from being in relationship with him.

I am fully aware that such subjective knowledge has its limits, especially for rationalists, who find certainty only in propositions and proofs. Yet I also began to discover an objective standard of truth about God. My primary source was the Bible, which I read from cover to cover, over and over again. Slowly, what I thought about God and human reality began to be shaped by the writers of the books of the Bible. For me their experiences translate into objective, concrete understanding. I also began to read other apologists, theologians, and devotional writers. I found myself rejecting their writings as often as I accepted them.

Almost imperceptibly, but with a snowballing force, one compelling fact emerged from this prayer and study: It was impossible to live a Christian life in isolation.

Why? Well, it was partly due to a growing awareness that in the being of God *himself* was the mystery of community. This is a mystery that can be apprehended if not comprehended, and has been adequately expressed only in the doctrine of the Trinity. Another aspect was the growing understanding that Jesus could be fully known only in fellowship with other people. This community could manifest itself in a variety of ways, from corporate worship to Bible studies, from prayer groups to ministries of witness and service.

When people first come to me for spiritual direction, I always ask why they are there. Of course they give me lots of different reasons, with responses ranging from eloquent clarity to inchoate confusion. Many, if not most, of these people express something to the effect, "My spiritual life is a wreck." When I ask them what that means, they almost inevitably respond by saying that they have lost any sense of meaning and discipline in private, personal prayer.

I quickly point out that personal prayer is only one component in the Christian life. To be in communion with God involves far more than just personal prayer. Christians can grow in intimacy with God in five ways: (1) through corporate worship or liturgy, (2) through nurturing fellowship with other Christians, (3) through studying the things of God, (4) through private prayer, and (5) through ministering to the needs of others. Nearly everyone who tells me that their "spiritual life" is in shambles is actually engaged already in one or more of these five areas.

THE THEOLOGY OF CHRISTIAN COMMUNITY

If I had to pick the one word in the New Testament that more than any other embodies what it means to be a Christian, the choice would be easy. It would be the Greek word *koinonia*, which has been translated into English as "communion," "fellowship," "intimacy," "participation," "sharing in common," or "giving to one another." *Koinonia* is something that happens only in a relationship between persons, when there is a mutual sharing. It is a sharing in something we don't already have, while giving to another something he or she doesn't already have. What is the something the other doesn't have? It is the self, the unique center of each person. The goal of Christian prayer is *koinonia* with God: fellowship, communion, intimacy with him. It is mutual. God shares his life, love, joy, and peace with us, and we give him what he doesn't have: our selves, our personal beings.

This *koinonia* was God's original intention in Creation. That is why human beings were created in God's image, so that we would receive the blessings of *koinonia*. It was *koinonia* that was lost in the Fall, when humanity rejected faithfulness to God in order to worship self. Cut off from God, the fellowship human beings could have with one another also became tainted with selfishness.

Koinonia is a uniquely Christian concept. The analogous word in Hebrew is *habar*, but that word is only used to describe relationships between human beings. In the Old Testament it is never used to refer to the relationship between a human being and God. Although certain patriarchs and prophets were called into powerful relationships with God, the stress was always on God's holiness and the awesome separation between God and his chosen people. Israel related to God through the covenant, a legal apparatus. No one, not Abraham, not Moses, not David, not Isaiah, no one could "see God face-to-face," and live.

In the revelation of the New Testament, that separation between God and humanity ended with the Incarnation of Jesus Christ. As the Evangelist John declared,

> In the beginning was the Word, and the Word was with God, and the Word was God. . . . And the Word became flesh and dwelt among us, full of grace and truth; we have beheld his glory, glory as of the only Son from the Father. (John 1:1, 14)

In the person Jesus of Nazareth, heaven and earth, divinity and humanity, joined together. Jesus Christ embraced humanity in order to liberate us from the selfishness, the sin, that separates us from God. He who was fully God became fully human, so that through him we could share in the life of God.

There are very few doctrinal statements in the Gospels. The theology of the Evangelists is implicit rather than explicit. Yet that early Christian community, that unremarkable, motley band of women and men, boldly proclaimed two things: *He is risen!* and *He is*

Lord! The basic Christian affirmation is, was, and will be "He is risen!" On Easter, God the Father raised Jesus of Nazareth from the dead. He was raised up to a whole new order of being. It was not a return, a restoration. It was not the restored innocence of the Garden of Eden. It was something entirely new, redemption, a completely new quality of intimacy with God. In Jesus Christ, a re-created humanity could share fully in the life of God.

This new quality of existence in Jesus is present in the Church through the Holy Spirit. Through the Church he calls women and men into this new existence through relationship with him. Yet relationship with Jesus is not an end in itself. It leads to a deeper mystery, with the realization that Jesus, too, is already in relationship.

Out of that mystery has grown the fundamental, definitive affirmation of Christian faith: God is eternally in *koinonia* within himself. God is not lonely, isolated, living in an eternal solitude. His very being is *koinonia*, in the relationship of the Father, Son, and Holy Spirit. The mystery of the Trinity remains just that: mystery. Yet it is a mystery that Christian women and men have experienced in the deepest moments of prayer. Even though it is seldom explicitly stated in the Bible, the Trinity is woven into its very fabric. In understanding the meaning of the New Testament, if redemption is the warp, the Trinity is the woof.

If the first theological affirmation in Christian history was "He is risen!" following immediately on its heels was the second, "He is Lord!" What exactly did the Apostles mean when they declared, "Jesus Christ is Lord!"? The Greek word for "lord" is *kurios*, and it was used in different ways in the first-century Mediterranean world. In Syria it meant the distinction between a cult god and his slavish devotees. In Egypt it was a title of the god who ruled the world. Throughout the Roman Empire it was used to refer to the emperor.

But for Jews it had a very unique, particular meaning rooted in the revelation of God's name to Moses through the burning bush. That name was *Yahweh*, which means, 'I AM WHO I AM" or "I WILL BE WHO I WILL BE." Jews, like nearly all ancient people, believed that a name embodied the very being of a person. For pious Jews, the name *Yahweh* was thus too holy to be spoken. So they referred to God, not just any god but the holy God who created and sustained the universe, as *Adonai*, which means "Lord." When the Hebrew Bible was translated into Greek in the Septuagint in the third century B.C., *Adonai* became *Kurios*. A Palestinian Jew in the first century would use the word *Kurios* to refer exclusively to *Yahweh*.

For the early Christian community, the statement "Jesus Christ is Lord" meant that Jesus Christ is *Yahweh*. So it was no accident that in the name of Jesus they prophesied, taught, preached, prayed, baptized, forgave sins, exorcized demons, and performed miracles. It was with clear-headed intentionality they claimed it was the name of Jesus in which all must believe, upon which all must call, in which they were cleansed, consecrated, and justified. For them the name of Jesus had the same comprehensive and pervasive meaning that the name *Yahweh* had in the Old

Testament. This view culminated in Paul's letter to the Philippians when he said,

> Therefore God has highly exalted him and bestowed on him the name which is above every name, that at the name of Jesus every knee shall bow, in heaven and on earth and under the earth, and every tongue confess that Jesus Christ is Lord, to the glory of God the Father. (Phil. 2:9–11)

However, neither the apostolic communities nor the Church down through history have taken for granted the claim "Jesus Christ is Lord." Because if Jesus Christ was truly human, if he really became a man, that claim includes an inequation. The New Testament already ascribed to another, to one completely other than Jesus of Nazareth, the true and genuine divinity as expressed in *Kurios*. Jesus was the Word, Jesus was the Son of God, but his dignity, lordship, and superiority were fundamentally other and subordinate to God the Father.

He did not proclaim his own kingdom, but the Kingdom of God. He called God the "one good" (Mark 10:18), and Jesus himself prayed to him. He distinguished between his own will and that of God (Mark 14:30), and he felt forsaken by God as he hung dying on the cross. Jesus even said that "the Father is greater than I" (John 14:28). He defined himself as an emissary of the Father, who lived to do the Father's will, speak the Father's words, and finish the Father's work. The goal of his life was not to lead people to himself, but to the Father (John 14:6). Obedience to the Father ultimately appeared to be the whole meaning of his calling and work. Somehow, all this evidence makes the claim "Jesus Christ is Lord" strike a false note.

Nevertheless, the New Testament witness concerning the relationship between God the Father and Jesus is incredibly powerful. The Word of God is utterly unique. It is not like other words that speak about God, or relate to God. For only this Word is in the place where the holy God himself is: in the beginning, before anything was created. As a matter of fact, the universe was created by the Word of God (John 1:1–3). The Word, in the very bosom of the Father, has revealed the invisible God.

Then comes the zinger: This Word became a human being and dwelt among us, full of grace and truth. This Word has been seen, heard, and touched (John 1:18). This Word, Jesus, is the heart of Christian proclamation, because God was in him, reconciling the world to himself (2 Cor. 5:19). In him the fullness of God dwells bodily (Col. 2:9). Reflecting on Jesus as the Word who existed before creation, and who will return at the end of time, the writer of the Book of Revelation wrote that he was the "alpha and omega" (Rev. 22:13), and the writer of the letter to the Hebrews that he was "the same yesterday, today, and forever" (Heb. 13:8).

Jesus himself proclaimed the unique unity between him and God the Father, saying,

Truly, truly I say to you, the Son can do nothing of his own accord, but only what he sees the Father doing; for whatever he does, that the Son does likewise. . . . The Father judges no one,

94

but has given all judgment to the Son, that all may honor the Son. (John 5:19, 22)

He also said, "I and the Father are one" (John 10:30), and "Know and understand that the Father is in me and I am in the Father" (John 10:38).

Yet the most remarkable claims about Jesus are found in the "I am" sayings. Many of these sayings of Jesus are very familiar to Christians. Teaching about himself, Jesus said things like "I am the bread of life," "I am the good shepherd," "I am the true vine," "I am the way, the truth, and the life," and others. In trying to understand the meaning of these sayings, most people put the emphasis on the object of the claims, such as, What does Jesus mean by "good shepherd" or "true vine"? But a closer analysis of the texts is very revealing.

The New Testament, of course, was written in Greek, which was the commonly held language from Spain in the west to the farthest stretches of Persia in the east. Jesus himself was most certainly trilingual. He would have spoken Aramaic to fellow Jews, and learned Hebrew in preparing for the responsibilities of a Jewish adult. Yet Greek was the dominant language in Galilee, where Jews and Gentiles lived in close proximity, and almost all commerce would have been conducted in Greek. Gentiles would have known only Greek, and Jesus spent important parts of his ministry with Gentiles, such as the Syro-Phoenician woman, and the people of Gadarea.

There is something most interesting in the grammatical structure of the "I am" sayings. In Greek, if you want to say "I am," you simply use the first-person singular of the verb "to be," which is *eimi*. It would be grammatically absurd to use a pronoun, because it is simply understood in the verbal form. Yet the "I am" sayings all begin with *ego eimi* (*ego* being the pronoun "I," and the root of the English word "ego"). Although grammatically nonsensical, the "I am" sayings take the emphasis away from the object, such as "the true vine," and powerfully place the stress on the subject.

What Jesus' listeners heard was "*I am* the good shepherd," and "*I am* the way, the truth, and the life." Jesus' meaning became crystal-clear when he said to the Pharisees, "Before Abraham was *I am*" (John 14:9). During his Passion, Jesus was on trial before the High Priest Caiaphas and refused to answer his questions. Finally Caiaphas asked him, "Are you the Christ, the Son of the Blessed?" Jesus answered, "*Ego eimi*, I am; and you will see the Son of man sitting at the right hand of Power, and coming with the clouds of heaven" (Mark 14:62). Caiaphas rent his robes, because he understood what Jesus had said. It was blasphemy. What Jesus was doing was claiming to be *Yahweh*, the great "I AM WHO I AM."

Jesus Christ is Lord. It means that he is fully God, but still distinct from God the Father. The mystery begins to open. There is a plurality of persons in the very being of God. God himself is a family. It is the Word of God who is the source of all revelation about God. That is the Son of God who is the point of contact between humanity and divinity. The Father remains hidden from human beings. As it says in the Gospel of John, "No one has ever seen God; the only Son, who is in the bosom of the Father, he has made him known" (John 1:19). Jesus said, "No one has seen the Father except him who is from God; he has seen the Father" (John 6:46). Jesus responded to a question of the Apostle Philip by saying, "He who has seen me has seen the Father" (John 14:9). The great revelation is this: *Jesus is Yahweh,* the revelation of God, the Word of God, God the Son, the Name above all names. The Father has always been hidden. The Father remains hidden. It was God the Son who called Abraham. It was God the Son who spoke to Moses through the burning bush. It was God the Son, the Word of God, who became flesh and dwelt among us. We know the reality of God only through God the Son.

Yet how do we know this? The mystery continues to unfold. We know that Jesus Christ is Lord because this revelation is brought to us, personally and intimately, by the Holy Spirit. Within the *koinonia* of God, there is a third person, the Holy Spirit. It is the Spirit who penetrates the being of women and men, enabling them to believe, and empowering them to enter into relationship with God. As Jesus himself told the Apostles,

> When the Spirit of truth comes, he will guide you into all truth, for he will not speak on his own authority, but whatever he hears he will speak, and he will declare to you the things that are to come. He will glorify me, for he will take what is mine and declare it to you. All that the Father has is mine; therefore I said he will take what is mine and declare it to you. (John 16:13–15)

The Apostle Paul wrote, "No one can say Jesus Christ is Lord except by the Holy Spirit" (1 Cor. 12:3). Now, if I were to get up from my desk right now, and go outside in front of my church, and stand on the street corner waving a hundred-dollar bill, saying to passersby, "I will give you this money if you say, 'Jesus Christ is Lord,'" I would be willing to bet you that same bill that nine out of ten people would make the declaration without batting an eye, fully without the assistance of the Holy Spirit.

That's not what Paul is talking about. What he means is that no human being has the ability *to believe* that Jesus Christ is Lord, and that no human being has the ability *to enter* the new life of grace in Jesus Christ, and no human being has the ability *to know* the mystery of the Trinity unless the Holy Spirit penetrates her or his being. As the Apostle John wrote, "In this we know that we dwell in him and he in us, because he has given us his Spirit" (1 John 4:13).

Although we can enter this new life now through the power of the Holy Spirit, its consummation remains apocalyptic. Don't worry, this doesn't mean the imminent end of the world. What it means is that the fulfillment of the Kingdom of God, the realization of this new existence, is a future event. We still live in a fallen, corrupt world, marred by injustice, violence, suffering, and death. We still struggle with our own selfishness and inability to truly love. The redemption we know now remains but a foretaste, a promise of what will be ours when Jesus comes again in judgment, when he will re-create heaven and earth.

Yet because of the Holy Spirit, Christian hope is not "pie in the sky." It is a future event that breaks into the present. The author of the letter to the Hebrews wrote that to participate in the Holy Spirit means to "have tasted the goodness of the Word of God and the powers of the age to come" (Heb. 6:5). St. Paul wrote that to be sealed in the Holy Spirit was "the guarantee of our inheritance until we acquire possession of it" (Eph. 1:14).

What does all this have to do with prayer? Every time we pray, we enter the future event of the Kingdom of God. All three persons within the being of God are involved in every prayer, yet even those who are blessed with the deepest intimacy only experience one person. That is part of the mystery. The Apostle Paul wrote about the inner dynamic of prayer in the eighth chapter of the letter to the Romans. Where does the desire to pray come from? The Holy Spirit, who has penetrated our being, gives us this need. How do we know what to pray? The Holy Spirit teaches us. As Paul says,

> Likewise the Spirit helps us in our weakness;
> for we do not know how to pray as we ought,
> but the Spirit himself intercedes for us with sighs
> too deep for words. (Rom. 8:26)

Who receives our prayer from the Holy Spirit? God the Son, at the behest of God the Father. The Apostle continues,

> And he who searches the hearts of men knows
> what is the mind of the Spirit, because the Spirit
> himself intercedes for the saints according to the
> will of God. We know that in everything God

works for good with those who love him. (Rom. 8:27–28)

The person who is known in the deepest intimacy of prayer is God the Son. The Holy Spirit does not draw attention to himself. He remains invisible. His function is to glorify the Son, so he invisibly directs all prayer to God the Son. The Son in turn receives our prayers and transforms them into his own. He then offers prayer for us to the Father. The Father remains hidden. We have no access to the Father, but the Son is in intimate relationship with him. So through God the Son, God the Father, who desires our good, receives our innermost prayers that have been searched out by God the Holy Spirit. The mystery of prayer, the mystery of the new life of redemption offered by the risen Lord Jesus Christ, is that we who pray thus enter into the communion within the Trinity. So the Christian life begins with this *koinonia*.

The Church reflects this *koinonia*. I would love to be able to say that the Church *is* this *koinonia*, but alas, the Church is part of both the fallen world and the redeemed new Creation. As an institution, the Church is clearly part of the world. Much within it is glorious. While kingdoms and nations have emerged only to disappear, while various dreams of grandeur have gripped the collective imagination of given societies only to turn into dust, the continuity of the Church's march across history is awesome in itself. The Church has inspired some of humanity's greatest offerings in art, music, and architecture. Historically the Church has been at the cutting edge of education, health care, and social reform.

Yet as an institution, the Church has been responsible for equal horror, supporting bigotry, hatred, social injustice, and even at times championing bloodshed. In its workings the Church is like any other human institution, so that political manipulation and savvy often lead to far greater success than does devotion, hard work, or intelligence. As the curate of a large parish, I spent most of my time on institutional maintenance, which has little, if anything, to do with the Kingdom of God. As the Swiss theologian Karl Barth said, the last great obstacle to the Kingdom of God on earth is the Church.

But, Dr. Barth went on to say, at the same time, the Church is also the place where God's Kingdom is most visibly manifest. From the perspective of the apocalyptic event of Jesus' Second Coming, and his creation of a new heaven and earth, the institutional nature of the Church, in both its glory and ignominy, is of little consequence. Through the eyes of Christ, the Church is *koinonia*. It is first of all *koinonia* between him and the Church. It is a relationship so close that Paul calls the Church "the Body of Christ." He is the head, and the Church is in relationship with him to perform his will (1 Cor. 12). Another image used to describe this intimacy is that the Church is "the Bride of Christ." The joyous, intimate love known between bride and bridegroom is the closest analogy to the *koinonia* that Jesus Christ calls us to.

THE LITURGY

Barbara and I went to church many times in the spring and summer of 1971. Feeling the need to be with other Christians, I was willing to try anything. We attended Congregational, Episcopal, Lutheran, even Pentecostal services. I didn't like any of them. I was hoping to experience the presence of God in a corporate setting, but I remained an outsider to whatever was going on in those places. The people were friendly, yet I couldn't penetrate the liturgies of the more formal churches, and the hysteria of the Pentecostals was disturbingly violent. I talked to some of the campus ministers. Although personally affirming, it was obvious my story made them nervous. None of them invited me to participate in their fellowships, but the Episcopal chaplain told me about the Madison Prayer and Praise Community, which met in his church on Saturday nights.

The first time we went, about a hundred people had gathered, sitting on the floor or in pews that had been pushed back along the edges of the room. They looked like people to whom I could relate, in their early twenties, most of the men with long hair and beards. There was a lot of hugging and touching and display of affection. A few people had guitars and began to sing songs praising Jesus. Everybody else knew the songs by heart and joined in. It seemed like there were no leaders, that the group moved from song to prayer to testimony to song with total spontaneity. The music and prayer swept me deeply and immediately into the presence of the Lord. The worship created a space that I was already familiar with. It was the place where day in and out I met Jesus. I was home, but for the first time with siblings.

After we became better integrated in the community I discovered that there were leaders, a group of about half a dozen who considered themselves elders. The times of worship on Saturday night were actually orchestrated with care, but in a way that allowed for absorption of the unexpected. Every worship service ended with a call to make a personal commitment to Jesus Christ. Over the two and a half years we were involved, dozens and dozens of young people responded. During warm weather a baptism by immersion in Lake Mendota behind the university student union would immediately follow.

After a short period I was asked to become part of the informal group of elders. At the time I had been serious about my Christian faith for just over a year. Few of the other "elders" had been renewed for much longer. We felt we were carrying forward the true work of God in the midst of an apostate and pagan city. A sense of self-important seriousness permeated our meetings. It is only in looking back that I am struck by the irony of calling ourselves "elders."

These young men first exposed me to the tensions of Christian community. Most of the regular members of the community were charismatic. They spoke in tongues, and focused on other "gifts of the Spirit" such as prophecy, healing, and ecstatic visions. In the fall of 1972 a split developed among us. The minority wanted the Saturday worship to be far more charismatic, manifesting the "gifts of the Spirit." The rest of the leaders, including me, felt that such worship would scare away the uncommitted and destroy opportunities for evangelism.

The more radical charismatics dropped out of the Saturday worship and began to gather on Sunday nights in the home of a language professor from the university. I was curious, so Barbara and I began to attend that service, too. It was a smaller group, of about thirty-five people, mostly adults but with a few children. The professor strictly controlled the flow of events. The evening consisted of speaking in tongues, prophecies, interpretations, and if anyone was ill, the laying on of hands for healing.

One night no one was ill, so they prayed for leg lengthenings. The professor said that almost everyone has one leg shorter than the other, which could cause lower back pain and other physical problems. He stood over me, measured my legs, and sure enough, my left leg was infinitesimally shorter than the right! A group laid their hands on the culpable leg, and as they prayed, I must admit I felt a power flow down it. The professor then told me my legs were perfect, just the way God had intended them to be.

Barbara hated the gratuitous leg lengthenings and other manifestations of self-absorption, and felt it was a massive ego trip for the domineering professor. He made me very uneasy as well. The last night I attended, the group was praising God. Everyone was singing in a different tongue, and it was jarringly discordant. But suddenly we were all swept into a beautiful harmony, a unity beyond description. It was as if we had been drawn into the heavenly host, as if in that moment heaven and earth met. I experienced an unspeakable peace and joy, while remaining very conscious of who I was and what was happening. I understood that if I stayed with them, I would have that experience many times. But I knew that was to be my last time. For many of those people their Christian identity was to be fulfilled in that little community. I was happy for them. But God was calling me along a different path. I had no regrets. My identity in Christ was elsewhere.

Later, when Barbara and I moved to California in order for me to enter Fuller Theological Seminary, our worship was drawn into the institutional Church. I worked in two Congregational churches, first in Hollywood and later in Claremont. The liturgies at both churches followed the normal Protestant pattern of centering on the sermon. The liturgies themselves, with hymns, Scripture lessons, formal prayers, and of course, a sermon, were boring. If the sermon was a dud, so was the entire time of worship. Since I was on the staff of those churches, for me worship became ministry. I was working more than worshiping. Yet I could still sense that God was there in a special way, even if remotely.

During my first year in California, I attended a conference for Congregational seminarians that was held at a Benedictine convent outside of Madison. The evening I arrived I'd noticed an arthritic old nun. It was difficult simply to watch her shuffle around with pain permanently etched on her face. The next morning I decided to go down to early mass, just to check it out. I sat directly behind the old nun. She was the first to go forward, and received the bread and wine standing up. When she turned to come back to her pew, she had the most beatific expression on her face that I have ever seen. In that moment I decided I had to discover what she'd experienced.

As I stood at the end of the line of communicants, I suddenly found myself assaulted by vile, obscene thoughts and visions. Now, I can conjure up some wild and crazy fantasies on my own, but these were far beyond anything I'd thought before. They came with the strong sense that I wasn't worthy to receive communion, that I should turn tail and return to my seat. But at the same time I knew that feeling was a lie. I knew that I had been redeemed by Jesus, and my worthiness resided in him. So I pushed forward through the filth in my mind. When I received the bread and wine from the priest, I encountered the risen Lord Jesus Christ in the most vivid way I had since the moment of my conversion. After that I began to seek out communion services as often as possible.

When we moved to Edinburgh in the fall of 1976, both Barbara and I wanted a neighborhood church that would feed us spiritually. We settled in at Morningside Baptist Church, one of the four churches on "Holy Corner." It was an interesting place. Their building had burned to the ground a couple of years before. The people had to decide whether to rebuild or simply disperse themselves among other Baptist churches in the area. While they were debating what to do, their minister transferred to a church in England. Though greatly dispirited, the congregation decided to rebuild and called another man to be their minister.

In the three years we were there, the church doubled in membership and became very vital spiritually. The minister was not a great preacher, and as I watched the church grow, I began to ask myself, why were so many newcomers there each week? One reason was strong lay leadership, particularly in pastoral care and personal evangelism. Another was the personal witness of the minister. To this day I haven't met a person who better manifested the love of God in his personality. I'm not joking when I say that even his welcome and announcements during the worship services were very redemptive.

But the unique thing about Morningside Baptist, for a Baptist church anyway, was that it had communion every Sunday. Over the months, I began to realize that the place where God's grace was being mediated in that community was not primarily in the proclamation of the Word in preaching and teaching and witness, but through the sacrament of communion.

About once a month at the Sunday evening service, we would have baptisms, by immersion, of course. The minister would climb down into the pool in the front of the sanctuary, and each adult would give a personal testimony before he or she was baptized. I would usually lead the communion service that followed. The power of the Holy Spirit, and the redemptive presence of the risen Lord were joyously palpable those nights. Slowly it began to dawn on me that the real treasure of the church was in the sacraments.

I began to spend time at the Anglican Community of the Transfiguration in Roslyn, outside Edinburgh. While there, I spent many hours discussing the meaning of the sacraments with one of the monks, Bishop Neil Russell. I came to understand, in some mysterious way, even though it demands faith for perception, God is objectively present in baptism and the Eucharist. Though invisible but to the eyes of faith, through baptism and the Eucharist the Christian community enters into an objective *koinonia* with God.

That growth in understanding was what led me to

leave the Congregational ministry and seek Anglican orders. Through further study and constant worship I began to understand the strength and power of the ancient liturgies of the Church that are in the Book of Common Prayer. The liturgies of the Church are about *koinonia*, with God and with each other. I particularly cherish the fact that the liturgies in the Book of Common Prayer are ancient. Christian men and women have prayed those same prayers for centuries. When we pray them, we not only enter *koinonia* with God and our neighbors, but in the mysterious power of the Holy Spirit we enter a *koinonia* with the communion of saints that stretches across the centuries.

It is of course obvious that corporate worship services can be excruciatingly boring as well as spectacularly beautiful. They can be starkly simple or rococo in complexity. Many times I find them so unengaging and tiresome, even when I am the officiant or celebrant, that I just go through the motions. Yet I know that even if, because of the thickness of my self-absorption, I am oblivious, God himself is present when his people gather to worship him. And over the years I have learned that the most constant element of my life with God is my regular involvement with the liturgy. When my personal discipline in prayer and study withers, when my fellowship with others becomes strained, when my ministry becomes a burden, when I enter a place of spiritual dryness, it is the liturgy that carries me, until in God's grace I enter again into a place of joyous intimacy with him.

I recently conducted a wedding for a couple who came from families that were only nominally Christian. Yet since both the bride and groom were committed Christians, they wanted to have a Eucharist in their service. They told me not to be surprised if very few if any of the family members and guests came forward. Nothing in the wedding liturgy seemed out of the ordinary, although the lessons were read with particular solemnity. But during the communion, the people just kept coming. Twice I had to consecrate more wafers. As I communicated the unexpected throng, I recognized that somehow, through the liturgy itself, those people had been touched by God. I hadn't done anything special; I was simply a character in the drama we were acting out together in the liturgy. The people gathered that day were bankers, teachers, doctors, social workers, homemakers, lawyers, all caught up in the events of their own lives. Yet through that wedding liturgy and Eucharist, they had been caught up in another drama. The one drama that really matters, the drama of the redemption of humanity by Jesus Christ.

FELLOWSHIP

It is impossible to be a Christian in isolation. My first months as a person of faith were difficult because I didn't know anyone who could understand what I was experiencing, or give me advice when I was confused or troubled. At that time Barbara's faith was in a different key than mine, and I was clumsy and obnoxious in sharing my experiences with her. She correctly felt I was trying to make her over in my image, and our spiritual conversations left us both frustrated and angry.

Yet I needed somebody to talk to, a connection in

the world, just to have the assurance that I wasn't crazy. The clergy I sought out were friendly enough (perhaps it would be better to say patronizingly bemused), but they had their own agendas of political action and campus ministry. Not one really understood what had happened to me. The Jesus people I knew were wildly apocalyptic, or fiercely moralistic, or both! They were always talking about the end times, and demanding radical changes in life-style under the threat of damnation. I wasn't interested in the apocalypse or moralism; I was interested in loving God. All I wanted was to talk with somebody else who knew him.

The first night Barbara and I went to the Madison Prayer and Praise Community I met a man named Bob Salinger. He stood out because he was a bit older than anyone else there, and far more conservatively dressed and groomed. He gave a little teaching on the Second Coming that was remarkable. Free of doom and gloom, and without judgment, his message that Jesus was coming again came across with matter-of-fact good humor. I remember thinking, how could someone as intelligent-sounding as he believe that Jesus is coming soon?

A secular Jew, Bob had become a Christian the year before in Ann Arbor through the Word of God Community, and had just moved to Madison to begin a psychiatric residency at the University Hospital. There was nothing formal about our relationship, but he, along with Frank Kaczmark, became the first of the many spiritual friends I have had over the years. Even if Bob hadn't had the same experiences as me, he always understood. He deflated my cosmic pretensions by making me laugh at myself, and kept me anchored in reality with his common sense. A spiritual shrink? Yes, and for me at the time, just the prescription I needed. A spiritual friend is a companion on the way, someone to share with, to pray with, to grow in Christ with.

Spiritual friendships may lead beyond companionship into accountability. During my first quarter at Fuller Seminary, I was arbitrarily assigned to meet weekly with some other new students in a fellowship group. We were to share our concerns and pray for each other. Four of us stayed together for three years, and from them I learned this important aspect of Christian fellowship: supportive accountability.

I was very insecure academically my first year, and was afraid to speak up in class in fear of making a fool of myself. Once, in a class on theology, I ventured to say something, and another student in the class insultingly ridiculed it. I was enraged, but too humiliated to respond. I met with my support group the following morning. Since two of the members had been in the class, I wanted their sympathy, and perhaps as a subtext, their help in planning some sort of appropriate revenge.

They were very unsympathetic. After we'd discussed the incident, and then prayed, they decided that the real spiritual problem was my anger. Then they decided that it was God's will for me to go to the guy who'd insulted me and seek his forgiveness for the vengeful rage I was feeling about him. On top of that, they gave me a deadline! I had to do this before we met again on the following Tuesday morning.

I didn't worry about it too much. I saw the guy a few times over the next couple of days, but there was still time. My friends in the group never said anything directly about my task, but whenever I was with one of them, we were aware of it. I tried to put it out of my mind until the next Monday, when there was no longer room to escape. At five-thirty on Monday afternoon I was sitting in the library, trying to study. I had to see my friends the following day, and I hadn't even tried. I prayed, to no relief. My friends were right; God wanted me to seek this guy out.

So on the spot I made a deal with the Lord. I would get up right then, walk across campus to the mail room, check my mail, and walk back. If I saw him, fine; I'd do what the group wanted. If I didn't see him, then I was off the hook. I began my walk with some anxiety, but as the campus was nearly empty, by the time I got to the mail room I was feeling easy. As I returned I could see no one in my path. I was free. I glanced in the student activities room as I sauntered by. There was only one person in the room. Shooting pool. It was he.

I would like to say that I went in and confessed my anger and the two of us had a wonderful reconciliation. What did happen was that I shot some terrible pool while I screwed up the courage to speak. When I did, he was surprised and coolly gracious. He hardly remembered the incident, but hadn't intended to insult me, and was sorry. Even though I continued to be wary of him, we did establish a kind of friendship, finding conversation easy from then on. What I learned is the importance of accountability in the Christian life. It is so easy to rationalize spiritually destructive behavior when we're isolated. I continue to listen for the voice of God to speak to me through someone I'm in fellowship with. To know and be known is part of the *koinonia* God intends for us in community.

There was a woman in my parish who suffered more physically than anyone I've known. As a young woman she had been a haute couture model and a singer with an operatic-quality voice. A degenerative arthritis slowly destroyed her joints, wracked her with excruciating pain, and left her crippled. She also developed a blood disorder that weakened her immune system, leaving her vulnerable to rampant infections, which caused short-term blindness and prolonged periods of acute nausea. She and her husband had deep faith, and in the midst of all her hospitalizations and medical attention, they never ceased to pray for her healing. Yet physical healing never came. Though her faith never wavered, more than once she said to me that God had abandoned her. "Where," she asked, "am I to see God's love for me?"

In her last years, she became the center of attention for a group of women in the parish. Most of them were a generation younger, and had gotten to know her through a women's Bible study and other parish activities. Singly or at times together, without any planning or organization, they simply began to visit her at home and in the hospital when she was there. They would run errands, care for some household duties, but mostly just be with her, pray with her, sit with her, talk with her. Slowly in the depth of her suffering, she began to realize that she had not been abandoned by God. True, there were no moments of mystical intimacy, or interventions of dramatic healing. The love of God came to her in a quiet way, through the calm, patient affection of those women. We cannot live the Christian life in isolation. He calls us into *koinonia*.

STUDY

Historically there have been thinkers who divided Christian revelation into three parts: the good, the beautiful, and the true. The *good* imposes itself as moral imperative, and was reduced by Jesus into the commandment to love. On the "Circle of Piety," (see page 57) the good would work itself out in a sensual spirituality. The *beautiful*, whether it be aesthetic or experiential, takes root primarily in the emotional realm of the circle. The *true*, on the other hand, is apprehended in the intellect, and manifests itself as doctrine and theology. Of course, these aren't airtight compartments, and they all inform one another. In Chapter 1, I have already discussed the relationship between personal theology and how one experiences the reality of God. Studying the things of God is critical in the Christian life as a way to grow in intimacy with him and in understanding how to live as a Christian.

There is no one way that Christians think. It can be argued that there are only three basic epistemological systems, or three basic philosophical systems that can be used to understand and explain reality. They are Platonism, Aristotelianism, and existentialism. Christian thinkers have used all three.

Plato (c. 427–347 B.C.) taught that the essence of reality was held in invisible, immaterial forms or ideals. Everything in the visible, material world is a mere shadow of the true, hidden ideal. Consequently, to apprehend the truth, a person must go beyond sense perceptions to contemplate the transcendent ideals. Platonism dominated early Christian thinking, and was worked into a systematic theology by Augustine of Hippo (354–430). It continued as a potent force in the Church right up into the twentieth century through the work of writers like C. S. Lewis.

Aristotle (384–322 B.C.) argued that truth could be arrived at through facts presented to sense perceptions, and logical deduction. The Dominican monk Thomas Aquinas (1225–1274) was the great Aristotelian systematizer in the Middle Ages. His thought has continued to dominate Roman Catholic orthodoxy in the contemporary world through twentieth century Neo-Thomists like Karl Rahner.

Existentialism is a system that believes truth can be known in human existence only through free acts of will. Blaise Pascal (1623–1662) and Soren Kierkegaard (1813–1855) were early Christian existentialists, and it was worked into a systematic theology by Karl Barth (1886–1968).

This discipline of study assumes that truth, and particularly truth about God, is both personal and objective. It is personal because Jesus himself is the "Truth" (John 14:6), and it is objective because he has particular attributes, and has revealed a particular plan of redemption in history. Consequently, Christian truth means that Christians view reality differently than non-Christians. For example, what is the truth about life after death?

In natural religions like Hinduism and Buddhism, and in occult spirituality, some sort of reincarnation or transmigration of souls is assumed. When I was involved in Eastern spirituality, I accepted the concept of reincarnation without giving it much thought. One day a close friend and I got off on a trip together. He had just returned from a lecture that had inspired a vision of the cycle of reincarnation. As we talked, we suddenly found ourselves on a high plane of consciousness, looking down at the world. We could see the whole pattern of reincarnation. The earth was at the center, and the spirits of thousands, if not millions, of human beings were flowing to and from various levels of consciousness and the earth itself, which was the material plane. (If you think this sounds Platonic, you're right!) It was beautiful, like seeing a living mandala. As we watched in awe, I suddenly realized something essentially false in it, and laughed out loud. The vision was shattered, and fell like broken glass all around us.

From that moment on I realized that ultimate reality had nothing to do with reincarnation. Neither did orthodox Christian thinking, which consistently taught that each human being was an utterly unique creation, given one life followed by death, followed by the resurrection of the body on the Day of Judgment. Over the years, as I thought about this issue, and talked with many people about it, I came to realize that any belief in eternal life is a matter of faith. It cannot be proven. But I believe the Christian understanding is true, and faith in reincarnation is false.

Why? Well, for one thing, I can't explain away my experience of the shattered vision. And for me, the evidence used to uphold reincarnation, such as "memory of past lives," has no imperative. I think such "proof" can be explained away as collective or genetic memory. But the real reason is that I believe the Christian gospel. God's plan of redemption, culminating in the incarnation, crucifixion, resurrection, and ascension of Jesus Christ, would be nonsense if reincarnation were true. Why would God himself have to come and die in our place if we human beings could work out our own salvation through the repeated effort of countless lives?

Why do I believe the Christian gospel? Because I have been given faith in it. My attitude is not anti-intellectual. I have two graduate degrees in theology, and feel I have a thorough understanding of both Christian and Hindu thinking. When I was an undergraduate I took a course called "Man, Religion, and Society." The "religious" systems we studied were Marxism and Freudianism. The professor was a self-avowed nihilist. Yet he often said the most perfect, seamless intellectual system ever created was that of Thomas Aquinas. The only problem was that a person had to believe in God to make it work. For my professor that was an insurmountable problem, because he had no faith.

One of my closest friends over the past twenty years is a man I first met in Madison when I was finishing my undergraduate work and he was in law school. Since then we have never lived in the same city, but we always managed to visit at least every other year. One of the brightest and best-read people I know, he is an agnostic bordering on atheism. Whenever we see each other, we always stay up the first night together until all hours, talking, arguing, laughing, usually about issues of faith.

Once, in Edinburgh, I was on a roll, explaining to him God's plan of redemption as it unfolded in human history. Suddenly, his face lit up in a way I'd never seen before. He began to repeat back what I'd been saying, interspersed with comments like, "That's amazing!" and "That is truly a thing of wonder!" Finally he paused, and then said, "You know, I've never really understood the Christian gospel before. It is the most amazing and beautiful thing I've ever heard. I don't believe it, but it sure is beautiful!"

Truth about the reality of God and redemption was established over centuries of conflict and struggle, and is encapsulated in the great creeds of the Church. This truth can be validly organized into different intellectual systems. Yet these systems are not ends in themselves. They become life-changing and redemptive only in the power of the Holy Spirit. For those who have been given the gift of faith, studying the things of God leads to a deeper intimacy with him. Studying the things of God prevents people of faith from chasing down blind alleys such as reincarnation. Studying the things of God allows people of faith to grow in understanding and appreciating the true, and beautiful, and finally the good.

MINISTRY

Koinonia with Jesus Christ ultimately means a mystical participation in all phases of his life. His life was one of loving service and giving to others, which culminated in his redemptive death on behalf of humanity. In union with Christ, as the Body of Christ, we continue his redemptive witness in a broken and suffering world, through prayer, prophecy, and service.

Jesus spent a great deal of time praying during his time on earth, and the second chapter of the letter to the Hebrews says that as the Great High Priest, he is in constant prayer for the world. As we pray, particularly as we pray for others, intimacy with him means that we enter his prayer. It means that our prayer is transformed into his prayer, and we discover his will for us in terms of our ministry.

When I began my doctoral work at the University of Edinburgh, my mentor, John McIntyre, insisted that I take three courses: the history of India, Hindu philosophy, and Sanskrit. After a couple of months of classes, I slowly felt impelled to make some sort of Christian witness to my fellow students. I began to pray every day that the Lord would create an opportunity for this. As I reflected on the situation, it made sense that the most receptive people would be in the Sanskrit class. I reasoned that the students in the history and philosophy classes were there because of some sort of deep interest in Hinduism, while those in the Sanskrit class were simply linguists. As time elapsed I wondered who the person would be I could share my faith with.

After a class on Hindu philosophy, on a cold, rainy December afternoon, I began to walk home across the Meadows with one of my fellow students. He was the most freaked-out of any in the class. Dressed a bit like a fakir, he was so involved in things Hindu that

I sometimes thought I could hear the faint whine of sitars in the background as he talked in class. It began to pour, and although we tried to share an umbrella, we both were getting soaked.

To my surprise, he began to tell me about his past. A British army brat, when he was nine he had gone with his mother to a Salvation Army revival meeting somewhere in Germany. At the end, the evangelist gave an altar call. He went forward and committed his life to Christ. He felt a new sense of joy, both because of his new faith and because his mother was so pleased. Later that same night, his mother died suddenly from a stroke. Sopping wet, chilled to the bone as we trudged along, he said, "Because of the cruel trick he played on me, from that moment I have hated the Christian God."

In the rain, I shared with him my faith. When it came time for us to part ways, he continued alongside me. When we arrived at my flat, we stood outside, huddled under the umbrella, our faces just inches apart, talking about the Passion of Jesus Christ. It was only then that it filtered through my thick skull that he was the one, the one God wanted me to be involved with. I invited him in, and as we drank tea and dried out, we prayed together. While fully aware that all kinds of conscious and subconscious factors contributed to our lives touching in this way, in my heart I know that left to my own devices, I would have avoided any contact. It was my prayer, mysteriously drawing me into the life and will of God, that created the situation.

Jesus Christ remains the one true missionary, seeking to restore prodigal sons and daughters to *koinonia*.

We are simply his agents, equipped for service through prayer. He remains the one true prophet, decrying the oppressor and succoring the oppressed. We are simply his instruments, emboldened and empowered through prayer. As prayer leads to intimacy with God which leads to ministry, ministry itself leads back into a unique kind of *koinonia*. As Jesus said in the Gospel of Matthew,

> Then the King will say to those at his right hand, "Come, O blessed of my Father, inherit the Kingdom prepared for you from the foundation of the world; for I was hungry and you gave me food, I was thirsty and you gave me drink, I was a stranger and you welcomed me, I was naked and you clothed me, I was sick and you visited me, I was in prison and you came to me." Then the righteous will answer him, "Lord, when did we see thee hungry and feed thee, or thirsty and give thee drink? And when did we see thee a stranger and welcome thee, or naked and clothe thee? And when did we see thee sick or in prison and visit thee?" And the King will answer them, "Truly, I say to you, as you did it to the least of these my brethren, you did it to me." (Matt. 25:34–40)

In all of these roles that grow out of *koinonia*, that of intercessor, witness, prophet, and servant, the continuing redemptive activity of Jesus himself interweaves through the ministry of the Church. In such ministry we discover our own identity in Christ. Every Christian has special and particular gifts. These gifts are never ends in themselves. They are for ministry both within and outside the Body of Christ. In the exercise of these gifts of ministry, God can be known in a way that is utterly unique.

For me, my special ministry is that of proclamation, in preaching and teaching. When I am in the pulpit, or with a class, I sometimes find myself becoming transparent, my mind and will one with that of God. I can't determine when it will happen, because it is solely through God's grace. Yet when it does, it is as if heaven has opened up all around me, as if I have transcended the temporal.

It comes through a giving of myself to God and to the people who are present. I feel as if I am dying to myself, becoming selfless, yet in the mystery of *koinonia* I know that in those moments of ministry I become most fully the person God has created me to be. It is not tied to specific ministries, but to whatever ministry an individual is called to. I have a friend who runs a feeding program at a church in Manhattan, and she tells me she feels the same reality as she ladles out soup to the men and women who come there to slake their hunger.

LIVING IN KOINONIA

We are called by God to be complete as he is complete, to be holy as he is holy. Why? So we can enjoy a more perfect *koinonia* with him. In all of these activities, of corporate worship, fellowship, study, and ministry, the Holy Spirit works through the activities themselves as well as through the discipline, sacrifice, and pain that may accompany them to purify us, to make us more holy, to prepare us to enjoy *koinonia* with God.

Our God is like a refiner's fire. In the ancient world, gold was refined through heat. A smelter would take the raw ore, put it in a pot, and build a fire under it. As the ore heated up, the impurities would rise to the surface, and he would scrape them off. He would then build an even hotter fire. More impurities would rise to the surface, and he would again scrape off the dross. He would make the fire even hotter and scrape off more impurities. The smelter would know that the gold was pure when he could look over the pot and see his own perfect reflection. In the same way the Holy Spirit refines us through a life of spiritual discipline. The goal is for Jesus Christ to look upon us and see a perfect reflection of himself. It is then we will enter fully into an intimate *koinonia* with God.

4

SPIRITUAL FRIENDSHIP

AFTER I HAD been renewed in faith for over a year I went through my first spiritual crisis. My new relationship with Jesus had of course radically changed my understanding of life. Things about myself that had never consciously bothered me before, then began to plague me. Foremost of these was lust. I felt that the Lord was calling me to a life of holiness, yet I was at times swept away by obsessive sexual fantasies. In my new faith, I believed that God had given me the ability to successfully deal with all my sins. I simply had to pray them out. So I would prayerfully meditate on my lustful desire, spiritually analyzing it, in the hope that when its foundations deep in my psyche were exposed, I would be able to root it out forever.

I would be successful for a while, and then fail miserably. My response was to redouble my efforts, only to fall again. After months of being caught in this cycle of strenuous hopefulness followed by abject disaster, I suddenly found myself questioning my faith. Was this all an illusion? What kind of cruel God would demand holiness, if he knew it was an impossibility? Who needed this kind of life? Yet at the same time I couldn't deny the presence of God in my life. I couldn't deny his love for me, nor my love for him. What could I do?

I called my friend Bob Salinger and asked to see him. He was in the midst of his residency in psychiatry at the University Hospital and had little time to spare. But he said he would meet me the following day on his lunch break. As we walked along the shores of Lake Mendota I summed up my frustrating confusion by saying that I felt as if the entire structure of my faith had collapsed in rubble all around me. He responded by saying, with a laugh in his voice, "Good." Taken aback and a bit irritated, I said, "What do you mean, good?" He stopped, looked me soberly in the eye, and said, "Good, Ken. Now maybe you'll let the Lord build something. What he builds will last forever."

I knew instantly that he was right. I had been trying to make myself holy through sheer effort and willpower, out of a fear of not measuring up. What I had never been consciously aware of until that moment, but which I immediately affirmed as true, was that I would *never* measure up through my own effort, and neither would anyone else. That's why we need a Savior. What took hold of me then was the understanding that I was to respond to God's demand for holiness by simply offering myself to him in confession and prayer. Any transformation, any growth in sanctification, would take place, often imperceptibly, solely in the context of my relationship with him. The power to change was not to be found in me. It would come solely from the Holy Spirit working mysteriously in our relationship.

I learned something else as a consequence of that conversation with Bob Salinger: how critically important it is in living out the Christian life to have a soul friend, a spiritual friend, a spiritual director. Bob was the first person with whom I could share my doubts, fears, and failures, as well as my insights, growth, and triumphs. A spiritual friend is one who will bring clarity to confusion, accountability when we stray, and at times in the mystery of grace, actually speak with the voice of God.

Why is it important to have a spiritual friend or spiritual director? Because the goal of the Christian life is to be in an intimate relationship with God, and it's not easy. In the first place, we are often afraid to really give ourselves over to God. We are accustomed to being in control of every moment. Entering the solitude necessary to hear the voice of God can be terrifying. But even more terrifying is the prospect that God will actually speak! Intimacy with God is not like any other relationship. It is being open to the awesome majesty of the One who is the Creator and Sustainer of the entire universe, the One whose holiness is so pure and severe it is like a refiner's fire. Perhaps as Israel in the Exodus, we will not want to follow where God is leading.

A life of intimacy with God calls us from living for ourselves to living for him and for others. Our self-centered pride does not allow us to go gently into the Kingdom of God. We remain extremely susceptible to willful self-delusion, and we are often unable to see how we deceive ourselves. At times like these, spiritual friends will not only hold us accountable, and help us to remain faithful, their companionship can calm our fears, and their prayerful guidance can help us to clearly discern the voice of God in the midst of our busy lives.

The way a person relates to a spiritual friend or spiritual director depends very much on his of her own particular emotional and psychological makeup and needs at a given time. Some people simply need a supportive companion on the way who will be seen when necessary. Others prefer a highly structured relationship with regular meetings, definite structure, and designated accountability. Often in spiritual direction, the director will design a discipline of prayer and study, and actually teach the other how to pray. In the history of God's people the entire scope of these relationships can be seen.

SPIRITUAL FRIENDSHIP IN HISTORY

Spiritual friendship is portrayed throughout the Bible. From the time he was a small boy, Samuel was trained in the things of God by the priest Eli. As a consequence of their relationship, Samuel grew to clearly hear and know the voice of God, and declare God's will to Israel. The great prophet Elijah, who stood for God against the apostate kings of Israel, raised up Elisha to carry on the voice of prophecy after his death. David and Jonathan offered each other support during times of crisis.

Of course, Jesus called out the twelve disciples to receive special teaching. Three of the twelve, Peter, James, and John, were given even more intimate instruction. The Apostle Paul tutored several young men, including Mark, Titus, and Timothy, in the

ways of the Lord. In some degree the Pastoral Epis-
tles, Paul's letters in the New Testament to Timothy,
Titus, and Philemon, can be seen as instruction in
spiritual direction.

In the fourth century, when Christians fled from
the corrupt Church into the desert in order to lead
lives devoted to God, their spirituality encompassed
a whole way of life. They did not practice an esoteric
doctrine or an ascetic discipline that could be taught
to another. For them prayer was offering every aspect
of their lives, body, mind, and spirit to God. In the
Apophthegmata, or *Sayings of the Desert Fathers*, it is written that when a monk seeking advice on prayer called
on Abba Lot, the venerable old man stood up, raised
his hands heavenward, and suddenly his fingers became like flames of fire. "If you only will," he said,
"you can become all afire."

The spirituality of the desert was not taught, but
caught. Consequently, the role of the "abba," of the
spiritual father, was of critical importance. Disciples
flocked to those who were perceived to be great men
of God in order to receive instruction. Yet it was not
doctrine or counseling they were after, but rather
something that would teach them about experiencing
the reality of God. Solitude was an important part of
their discipline, so there was an economy of words in
the exchanges between the abbas and their disciples
that seems almost comical to us. A monk once came
to Basil the Great and said, "Speak a word, Abba,"
and Basil replied, "Love the Lord your God with all
your heart," and the monk immediately left. Twenty
years later the monk returned and said, "Abba, I have
struggled to obey your word; now give me another,"

and Basil replied, "Love your neighbor as yourself," and the monk returned with it to his cell.

As the Middle Ages unfolded, a great pietistic division in the life of the Church developed. Those who wished to be devoted to God became priests, monks, or nuns, while the involvement of the laity was often reduced to attendance at the Sunday mass. Even that participation was minimal, as the Latin liturgy retreated in mystery behind the barriers of new vernacular languages. The people may have learned the Latin Lord's Prayer, Creed, and Confession, but without knowing what they were saying. Devotion to the Eucharist remained widespread, however, as the mystery of salvation was acted out in a tangible, tactile way.

The thirteenth century brought about a great desire for renewal among the laity. Francis of Assisi felt that personal intimacy with God was available to all people. He developed a life of prayer, which he taught to his lay followers, that focused on an imaginative meditation on the Nativity and Passion of Christ. Another great reformer and contemporary of Francis, Dominic (1170–1221), founded the Mendicant Order of Preachers to combat heresy among the laity. Dominic worked to break down the pietistic barriors between clergy and laity, insisting that every Christian should have spiritual direction, and he trained lay spiritual directors. Yet renewal among the laity was short-lived.

In the eyes of many fourteenth- and fifteenth-century Christians, the Church in Western Europe had sunk into a morass of corruption, immorality, and laxity. The clergy were often ignorant, impious, and lazy.

Cut off from the liturgy by the Latin language and priestly domination, the common people had little understanding of the central facts of the gospel, or of Jesus Christ's personal presence in the sacraments and proclamation. Popular piety became obsessed with superstitious devotion to tangible mediators of salvation such as relics, icons of the saints, and even the blessed sacrament itself.

In reaction to a church debauched with corruption, as well as the false mysticism shot through with monism which had sprung up all over Europe, Gerard Groote (1340–1384) began another ministry of renewal. Born into a wealthy Dutch family, he was a brilliant scholar set on the path of high ecclesiastical office. However, in 1377 a strange thing happened. He met the living Lord Jesus Christ and had his life transformed. After refusing ordination to the priesthood, Groote became a deacon so he would be allowed to preach. He championed a realistic, practical discipline of prayer which became known as the *devotio moderna*, or modern devotion. It was based on an emotional commitment to imitate the humanity of Jesus, with the goal of growth in virtue and active charity. Many of his lay followers were organized into the Brethren of the Common Life, and adopted a communal practice of prayer, meditation, and work. *The Imitation of Christ*, written by one of Groote's followers, Thomas à Kempis (c.1380–1471), has proven to be so popular historically, there are more copies of it in print than any other book but the Bible.

Of course, one of the powerful consequences of the Protestant Reformation was a tremendous outburst of lay commitment. One great dictum of the Reformation was the priesthood of all believers. Given access to the Bible in their vernaculars, lay Protestants developed a life of piety that was built around the Word of God. In reaction to the Protestant Reformation, the sixteenth century also saw one of the great flowerings of Roman Catholic spirituality. The Spanish School, which was rooted in Groote's *devotio moderna,* produced three giants who still speak with tremendous influence and power to a wide readership at the end of the twentieth century. These three, Ignatius Loyola, Teresa of Avila, and John of the Cross, desired to reduce the principles of prayer to a science that could be taught to the whole Church, both clergy and laity.

Born into the Basque nobility, Ignatius Loyola (1491–1556) was as a young man captured by the romantic ideals of knighthood and martial glory. He became a soldier, and in 1521, during a war between Spain and France, his left leg was shattered by a cannonball. During his long convalescence he read and reread a book on the life of Christ, and another on the lives of the saints. Seized by a new ideal, Ignatius decided to become a soldier for Christ. After making a pilgrimage to the monastery of Montserrat near Pamplona, he walked to Manresa, where he spent a year living as an ascetic, devoting himself to prayer and reflection. Suddenly enlightened during prayer, he realized that the Church as the body of Christ was called to continue Jesus' ministry of redemption in the world.

In 1526 he went to study at the University of Alcala, and gathered a small group of followers to whom he taught the discipline of prayer. His book *Spiritual Ex-*

ercises was based on Ignatius's own conversion and life of prayer during that year at Manresa. Two years later, he went on to the University of Paris to complete his theological education. On August 15, 1534, Ignatius and six companions (including Francis Xavier) met in the church on Montmartre to take vows of poverty, chastity, and obedience, not in order to lead a life of contemplation, but as the foundation of a life of ministry. In 1540 this new religious order was approved by the Pope as the Society of Jesus. The Jesuits (as they were called) took a fourth vow, that of "unhesitating obedience to the orders given by the Pope for the salvation of souls and the propagation of the faith."

Although the influence of the Jesuits as missionaries, educators, and advisers to kings and princes was enormous, history may show that the impact of Ignatius's *Spiritual Exercises* has been even greater. It was not a book to be studied, but a concrete, personal experience to be entered into over a period of four weeks, leading to deeper intimacy with God. Ignatius warned that contemplation consisted of two parts: "consolation," which was love present with conflicting emotions such as joy and terror, or bliss and sadness; and "desolation," which was a darkness of the spirit accompanied by great temptation. The five methods of the exercises were designed to move the person in prayer from active to receptive modes of consciousness. This prayer consisted of reflection tied either to the rhythms of breath or to the imaging of biblical scenes. More than anything else, these exercises open the human imagination to the redemptive presence of God.

The desire for reform within existing orders also

took root in Spain. Teresa of Avila (1515–1582) lived a very comfortable life in the large Carmelite convent in the Castilian town of Avila. Loving, vivacious, and charming, Teresa was a favorite not only in the convent, but in the social life of the town. She herself was deeply troubled by the luxury and spiritual aridity of her life. In 1555 she began to experience a series of rapturous visions which led to a "second conversion." She realized four stages of prayer: discursive meditation, emotional recollection, God's presence in "quiet," and finally, in "union" or "marriage."

With a few other nuns she founded a new house of "discalced" ("barefoot") Carmelites dedicated to prayer, physical penance, and poverty. In the face of often hostile opposition she traveled Spain to found and nurture other discalced communities. Her writings were filled with grace, humor, psychological insight, and a remarkable balance of mystical vision and common-sense practicality. She herself told the story that she was once on an arduous journey to a remote convent riding uncomfortably in the back of a horse-drawn cart when it suddenly tipped, sending her sprawling into a muddy puddle. Still sitting in the mire, she raised her fist to heaven and muttered, "If this is the way you treat your friends, it's no wonder you have so few!"

In 1567 Teresa met a young Carmelite monk who agreed to assist her in bringing reform to their order. This young man, who later took the name John of the Cross (1542–1591), suffered imprisonment and torture in spite of the gentleness of his reforming zeal. Like no one before or since, John was able to tenderly and lovingly express the fierce demands of the holy

God. For John there were three steps toward God through prayer. The first was "purgation" through what he called the "dark night." The dark night of the senses led to a free renunciation of all inordinate appetites and prideful cognition. *The Dark Night of the Soul,* his major work, described in spatial terms that place where the Christian suffered alienation, isolation, and the inability to pray, which led ultimately to "betrothal" or "illumination," before reaching the goal of "union with God."

A generation later a Frenchman, Francis de Sales (1567–1622), attempted to combine elements of Ignatian and Carmelite spirituality into a discipline of prayer that could be tailored for use by anyone in any profession or stage of life. In many ways the Spanish school of spirituality was a reaction to its time. A reaction not only to the demands for reform, but also in an age of reason, an attempt to create a science of the spiritual life. It was a systematic analysis of the experience of prayer, with the aim of describing both the means and end of prayer in a way that anyone could learn and teach to others.

Yet at the same time it emphasized the subjective side of prayer. More attention was paid to mental and emotional reactions than to the object or objective content of prayer. One consequence of this was the emphasis on prayer not as an end in itself, but as the source of power for ministry. Another consequence was a gradual depreciation of the liturgy in the life of a Christian. Personal prayer, and personal spiritual growth, became more valuable than living a life in submission to the discipline of the Church's liturgical offices.

Although Protestant piety for the most part developed along independent lines from the modern devotion, one of the greatest spiritual geniuses in all of Christian history felt free to draw from all sources. John Wesley (1703–1791) was the fifteenth child of the Anglican priest Samuel Wesley and his wife Susannah. He was raised in a home of deeply disciplined piety. As a young man studying at Oxford University, he became intensely dissatisfied with both the lack of personal spiritual reality in the Anglican Church and its failure to reach out to the lower classes. His reading led him under the influence of the *devotio moderna* though the work of à Kempis, Loyola, Teresa of Avila, and Francis de Sales. He coupled that with a rationalistic and moralistic Anglican discipline championed by Jeremy Taylor and William Law, 17th century Anglican Divines. In 1729 he gathered a group of young men who met every evening for either study, prayer, worship, or ministry to the sick or prisoners. At first dubbed "the Holy Club," because of the regularity of their observances, the group later became known as the "Methodists."

After ordination to the priesthood, Wesley sailed to the colony of Georgia in 1735. The negative reaction by colonists to his punctilious insistence on liturgical correctness and legalistically inflexible moralism resulted in the total failure of his ministry. Disheartened, he returned to England in 1737 and began to worship with the Moravian Brethren. The following year, while listening to a reading of Luther's *Preface to the Epistle of the Romans,* he suddenly encountered the living, redemptive presence of Jesus Christ. The claims of the gospel were no longer just universal, abstract truths. He then knew that Jesus had died to save him, John Wesley, and wrote that "his heart was strangely warmed." He devoted the rest of his life to bringing this conviction and experience to others.

Meeting hostility from the reserved, upper-class, rationalistic Anglican hierarchy, Wesley began to preach in the open air to large crowds of the working class. It is estimated that over the next fifty years he traveled over two hundred thousand miles and preached over forty thousand sermons. He was also a brilliant organizer, and created a structure of lay preachers and cell groups devoted to the Christian life in three steps: *justification* through baptism, *redemption* through the personal experience of salvation, and *sanctification* through a life of disciplined holiness under the guidance of the Holy Spirit. Wesley proclaimed that everyone who accepted Jesus Christ would be saved, and that the Holy Spirit would bless those who seriously sought holiness with complete deliverance from the power of sin.

When Anglican bishops refused to ordain untrained lay Methodists to the priesthood, Wesley, convinced that there was no biblical distinction between bishops and priests, began to ordain "superintendents" to oversee the work of renewal and outreach in America and Scotland. Consequently, Methodism split from the Anglican communion and became an independent Protestant denomination.

Although Protestantism remained moralistic and revivalistic, the development of disciplined spirituality tended to become goal-oriented, especially as the foundation for evangelism. The Englishman William

Booth (1829–1912) organized the Salvation Army to bring the gospel to the poor in urban slums. His style of evangelism was highly appealing, using colloquial language and popular music, yet those who responded were drawn into a very tightly disciplined life of prayer, study, and ministry. Every member of the Salvation Army became an evangelist.

Almost a century later, Bill Bright (1920–), who had been a successful candy manufacturer, felt called to begin a ministry of evangelism at colleges and universities. In 1951 he founded Campus Crusade for Christ at the University of California in Los Angeles. Bright reduced the call to Christian commitment to *The Four Spiritual Laws,* which could be easily presented and understood in the context of personal evangelism. Those who joined Campus Crusade entered a highly structured program of prayer and study, which was intended to become the basis for further lay evangelism. Remaining a lay movement, Campus Crusade has produced thousands of young people eager for ministry, not only on campuses, but since the 1980s in dozens of urban areas and foreign countries.

For me, my friend B. J. Weber is a model for spiritual friendship. His life is essentially built around a commitment to personal evangelism. For several years he worked in the Times Square area of Manhattan with what he called our society's rejects: prostitutes, pimps, drug addicts, runaways, the homeless. Recently he has begun focusing more of his attention on leaders of New York's business community, in order to represent the poor to them.

When B. J. takes someone into spiritual direction,

he makes himself totally available. He will meet with them several times a week, before work, at lunch, in the evening, to talk to them about what it means to be a Christian, to study the Bible, and to teach them to pray by praying with them. He'll work out with them, go to the theater with them, even hang out in bars with them, until they are solidly established in their own relationship with God. Then he will see to it that they get involved in a parish church, and a small fellowship group, as well as some sort of ministry. He will remain available to them if they have any need, any time of day or night. When B. J. and I get together, he might begin by saying, "Tell me what holiness is," and we'll be off on two hours of absorbed conversation, prayer, and often a blessing of grace. He is someone who gives his life to others so that they might enter the life of God.

FINDING A SPIRITUAL DIRECTOR

Finding someone who can teach about more fully entering intimacy with God is not easy. More often than not a spiritual director will be a layperson. A few seminaries have begun offering courses in spiritual direction, but most ignore the issue. So what qualities should you be looking for? Theodora, one of the great female ascetics of the desert, gave a good summary when she said,

> A teacher ought to be a stranger to the desire for domination, vain-glory, and pride; one should not be able to fool him by flattery, nor blind him by gifts, nor conquer him by the stom-

ach, nor dominate him by anger; but he should be patient, gentle and humble as far as possible; he must be tested and without partisanship, full of concern, and a lover of souls.

In many ways Theodora's criteria are similar to those that the Apostle Paul listed for bishops in 1 Timothy 3. A spiritual director should be someone emotionally secure, self-controlled, and sober, who will be able to maintain an objectivity in the relationship. For the Desert Fathers and Mothers, one of the primary virtues was *apatheia*. This Greek word passed into English as "apathy," but that is not at all what it meant to them. It connoted "detachment" and "disinterest," but its primary meaning was "temperance" or "sobriety" or "self-control" or "orderliness." Or, if you like, "freedom." *Apatheia* meant to be set free from compulsion, obsession, and self-absorption in order to love another. In looking for a spiritual director, avoid at all costs someone who is doing it for his or her own ego gratification. Also, avoid entering spiritual direction with someone easily manipulated by flattery or gifts. Look for a person who has nothing to gain from the relationship, who will take it on reluctantly.

A good spiritual director or spiritual friend should also manifest what in Galatians 5 and Colossians 3 the Apostle Paul calls the "fruit of the Spirit," things such as patience, kindness, goodness, faithfulness, gentleness, lowliness, and meekness. Look for someone who is in touch with his or her own sinfulness and has experienced God's grace and forgiveness. Look for someone who knows what it means to be broken, and has compassion, not judgment, for the weaknesses of others. People who know it all, who have all the answers, who take themselves most seriously, are the worst spiritual directors. Humility is the key, a humility that enables people to accept themselves, love themselves, and laugh at themselves.

Spiritual directors should be a people of learning. They should be comfortable and familiar with the Bible. Athanasius wrote that Antony of Egypt, the greatest of the Desert Fathers, knew the entire Bible by heart. Father William told me that many of the early monasteries required their novices to memorize the Psalms, the Gospels, and other biblical books before they were given final vows. Spiritual directors should also understand the importance of theology, and be well versed in the central doctrines of the Trinity, Creation, Incarnation, Atonement, and Sanctification. It is helpful if they have a "catholic" spirit, and don't try to impose their own theological particularities on others. Teresa of Avila wrote that "the devil has an enormous dread of that learning which has the company of compassion and humility."

Perhaps the most important quality is to find a person who loves God, and manifests that love in an active discipline of prayer. Look for a person who takes his or her own counsel. What could be more ludicrous than to be in spiritual direction with someone who doesn't pray himself or herself! Don't laugh, it can happen! Look for a person who can talk about his or her own experiences in prayer, who has wrestled with God in prayer, and has struggled with the demands of living a disciplined life of prayer. The most helpful spiritual friend is one who is able to mediate the presence of God personally rather than intellectually. Obviously people who manifest *all* these qualities are difficult to find. I've never met one. If you do, call me. I'd like to ask him or her to become my spiritual director.

Father William's first spiritual director at New Melleray Abbey was a monk of great learning named Father Sean. As a younger man he had been a Jesuit of high rank, and he had held positions of power in the Roman Catholic Church far, far beyond any of the other monks at New Mellerary. At the time Father Sean was suffering from a heart condition, and would invite William into his room in the infirmary. He would pray out loud and let William simply witness how he related to God. William can still repeat those prayers. "O Jesus," Father Sean would pray with passion, "I love you. I love you. O Jesus, have compassion on those who don't know you. Come to them. Come to those who are suffering. Touch them with your peace. Jesus. Jesus." He would turn to William and say, "Do you understand?" Slowly, as William learned to pray with the same direct simplicity, he was drawn into the same passion, the same love.

DIFFERENT KINDS OF SPIRITUAL FRIENDSHIP

Whatever a person calls it, spiritual friendship, spiritual direction, or discipleship (the favored Protestant term), the relationship where one Christian teaches another about intimacy with God can manifest itself in a variety of ways. The most common form is a spiritual companionship of total mutuality. I have been involved in several of these relationships. My soul friends and I will schedule a regular time to meet, usually once a week. The format will vary, but most often it entails some study of a passage of Scripture or other reading we are both doing, a time of sharing immediate concerns, culminating in prayer with and for each other. The mutuality of such relationships is found in the fact that leadership or direction often passes back and forth depending on the circumstances of the day.

For me these relationships have a triple value. Not every Christian has every one of the spiritual gifts. That is one reason we are called into fellowship, because all the gifts are present in the gathered community. I have often been told by my friends that when it comes to myself, I do not have the gift of discernment, which means knowing God's will. I sometimes have it for others, but almost never for myself. Discernment often fails me when I desire something for selfish reasons, and then rationalize that it is what God wants, too. When I am confused about what God's will for me is, I can ask one or more of my soul friends to help me discern it.

These spiritual friendships demand a total openness, a complete transparency before the other. Of course, this can only happen in a context of trust and confidentiality. Consequently, a second value in them is accountability. Not infrequently, I will find myself caught up in a self-destructive impulse or in some sort of compulsive inner imperative. When I know I will be seeing a spiritual friend in the next few days, and will have to tell him or her about it, I will often have the ability not to act rashly. When we do meet and I share what's going on, I know that my friend will help me pray in order to both discover God's will and receive the strength to follow through on it.

The times I must confess to them that I have behaved in a hurtful and ungodly way, I know that they will not reject me, but will be there for me. For me, not for my behavior. Again, they will help me pray, both to discover God's will in terms of reconciliation or restitution, and to receive from God the courage to act on it. This kind of accountability helps me, as it helps them when they're in need, to keep my life oriented toward God and others. Without these relationships it would be very easy for me to hide myself, and keep myself cut off from his Kingdom.

Another kind of spiritual friendship has much more of the quality of a teacher and student relationship. This is where one of greater knowledge and experience imparts what he or she knows about God to another. In classical writings on spiritual direction the imagery used to describe this kind of relationship is that of a gardener tending flowers, or a nurse caring for a patient. I have been involved in many of these relationships, too. Twice I have taken the role of student, both times with Roman Catholic monks, Daniel Morrissey, a Dominican, and William Wilson, a Trappist. Many times I have taken the role of teacher, always with people who have sought me out.

Father William has taught me a tremendous amount about this kind of spiritual relationship. In a sense it demands a transfer of a person's center of dominion and authenticity from self to another, but it cannot be mechanized or made permanent. It is only for here and now. It is not submission to a higher authority, as in the Church to bishops and abbots. No, it remains a friendship. It is not a law or necessity, it is a *charism*, a gift. The hope is that we will have a "one-on-one" encounter with Jesus Christ, through another person. In a sense, spiritual direction is thus sacramental. Just as Jesus Christ comes to us, is immediately present to us in the bread and wine of the Eucharist, the hope is he will come to us and be immediately present to us in the spiritual director.

But this relationship is temporary. The director is constituted spiritual father or mother through an act of faith by the disciple. He or she is constituted, maintained in being, and dissolved as spiritual father or mother on the act of faith of the disciple. So the teacher in this relationship will never be superior to the student. The spiritual director must annihilate self in the relationship, the way a priest becomes transparent in celebrating the Eucharist. The director must say, "I am nothing. He makes me spiritual father for him." So the center, the red-hot center of spiritual direction, is the passionate pursuit of the will of God, making use of this means that God has provided. The hope is that today, the director will speak with the voice of Jesus Christ.

The director must assume certain obligations. Foremost is the commitment to care for the others during this portion of their walk with God. It is not rooted in emotion, but rather in a willful commitment to their well-being. It is a commitment to pray for them as for self. The director must be available to them, but never expect them to come for consultation. When they do come, they must never be obligated to follow the director's advice. The advice is a pure offering, a gift, a *charism*.

There are those who feel that the relationship between director and disciple should be like that of master and slave, with the disciple giving the director complete, unthinking, blind obedience. I totally reject that as unbiblical and utterly alien to the way God himself relates to us. Jesus Christ came to set us free. Free from our sins, free from our compulsions, free to serve and obey him, yes. But it is a service and obedience that is a free offering of love, not something taken on in the hope of a reward.

Christian spiritual direction is utterly different than the relationships of Eastern masters and their devotees, where blind obedience is offered in order to ultimately earn some sort of "black belt." The Christian spiritual director must be constantly on guard to be sure that the disciple is not using the relationship to avoid growth in autonomy, independence, and decisiveness. The ultimate goal of the spiritual director is to put himself or herself out of business, so that the disciple will be able to walk with God on his or her own.

WHAT SPIRITUAL DIRECTION IS NOT

Spiritual direction is not confession. For Catholic Christians confession is a sacrament, the acknowledgment of specific sins in the context of repentance and penance, followed by the reception of absolution from a priest. Confession is an important, crucial part of my life with God. It may often be part of a relationship of spiritual direction, but it is not a necessary component. I take special care to separate the two. I have a confessor, whom I see three or four times a year. The advice he gives me has been wonderfully important in shaping my life with God, and is integral to my well-being as a Christian. As a parish priest I often hear people's confessions. Sometimes, under very special circumstances, I will hear the confession of someone I have in spiritual direction, because it can be helpful in the person's learning about God. But if someone I have in direction wants to make a confession, I encourage him or her to go to another priest, because it is best not to confuse the two disciplines.

Spiritual direction is not counseling. It doesn't have to do with crisis management or resolution of specific problems. Spiritual direction concerns nurturing a person's relationship with God. There are times when a personal crisis overlaps with someone's spiritual life, and then it is appropriate to deal with it. But I have learned spiritual friendship can very easily degenerate into counseling when specific problems are the focus. Concentrating on problem resolution also tends to foster a dependent relationship, which is the opposite of the goal of spiritual direction or spiritual friendship. If personal problems are continually being brought up, I will refer the person to someone else for counseling. This may cause hurt feelings at first, but as a parish priest I have neither the time, the inclination, nor the training to work with someone who needs professional help.

Spiritual direction is not psychotherapy. I understand the goal of psychotherapy is to make the unconscious conscious. Unconscious impulses often re-

sult in compulsive, obsessive, neurotic, or even path-
ological behavior, and many people who are unhappily
locked into self-destructive patterns don't even know
why they behave the way they do. Psychotherapy
helps people to break into their unconscious so they
will understand why they feel and act as they do. The
intention is that once these unconscious impulses become known, they will lose the power to dictate blind
behavior.

The work in depth psychology by Sigmund Freud,
Carl Jung, and others has changed the way people
think about prayer. This is because psychoanalysis has
put a structure on the human psyche that can be very
helpful in understanding what is happening when
people pray. Some Christian writers, such as John San-
ford and Morton Kelsey, have even attempted to re-
constitute the reality of prayer in Jungian terms. Ultimately they fail because Christian spirituality can be
reconciled to Jungian monism only at the sacrifice of
the former.

I find the insights of psychoanalysis beneficial for
prayer. Entering a discipline of prayer opens up the
unconscious, and the patterns of depth psychology can
provide a map to this often unfamiliar territory. Very
often people who begin a life of prayer get in touch
with parts of their psyche that are difficult for them
to integrate. Again, I am not trained, nor do I have
the time, to help people deal with some of these issues. So when this happens, I will refer them to psychotherapy. I work with a group of Christian psycho-
therapists (some of whom I have in spiritual direction),
and we have discovered that our combined work with
a particular person will help him or her achieve both

emotional and psychological integration, as well as growth in relationship to God.

WHAT HAPPENS IN SPIRITUAL DIRECTION

The Dutch priest Henri Nouwen has written that spiritual direction can be understood as moving a person from self-absorption and self service to an attitude of listening to and becoming obedient toward God. For Nouwen, this movement has three parts. The first is to encourage a person to enter the discipline of worship in the Church. This is because the calendar of the liturgy presents over each year the full meaning of Christian redemption: Jesus is being born at Christmas, Jesus manifests himself to the world in Epiphany, Jesus is suffering and dying in Lent, Jesus is raised up in Easter, Jesus is ascending to heaven in Ascension, Jesus is sending the Holy Spirit in Pentecost, Jesus is coming in Advent. Living in the Church thus enables us to see the divine events that underlie and control history, and which will give meaning to our own lives.

The second task of spiritual direction for Nouwen is to encourage people to enter the discipline of the Book. This means to search out and listen in a very personal way to the Word of God as it comes to us through the Bible. Remember that the Word of God is Jesus Christ. He is personally present in and among and behind the words in the Bible. As we listen we begin to recognize his voice speaking directly to us, calling us to obedience. Meditation on Holy Scripture allows the Word to pass from our minds into our hearts, in order to reshape our very being. So in a very real way, meditation on the Word of God becomes part of the ongoing Incarnation of God in the world.

The final task of spiritual direction in Henri Nouwen's understanding is what he calls the discipline of the heart, which is learning how to pray in such a way that we offer our entire being to God. One consequence of this prayer is self-knowledge. The difficulty in developing this kind of prayer is that our natural tendency is to relate to God the way we relate to other people, presenting only what we think will elicit a positive response. So our prayer life becomes as narrow and selective as our other relationships. We remain strangers, before God, before others, and before ourselves.

The discipline of the heart demands giving everything to God: our fears and sorrow, our greed and envy, our anger and violence, our gluttony and lust, our sloth and pride, our hopes and dreams, our fantasies and aspirations, our joys and triumphs, our work and leisure, our family, friends, and enemies, everything, everything that we are. And as we offer our total being to God, we must learn to *listen* to his voice, and allow him to speak to every part of us.

When a person comes to me seeking spiritual direction, I will usually take at least two sessions, about an hour each, simply getting to know him or her. I will only agree to see the person twice. After two meetings, we can make a mutual decision whether to continue. The intended movement in spiritual direction as articulated by Henri Nouwen is extremely demanding. So I want to discover whether a person seriously desires to give his or her life to God, or whether the motive is simply a dilettantish dabbling.

Often people don't know the reason themselves. They come to me desiring direction at all stages of spiritual maturity. So I need to find our exactly what their experience has been in the Christian life. During a first session I will ask about their background: parents, siblings, marital status, family responsibilities, places lived, education, work, hobbies, and involvement with the church. I will also ask them why they want to be in spiritual direction, and how much time a week for worship, prayer, and study they are willing to commit.

A second session will usually take place two weeks later. During the interim, I will have asked them to prepare a spiritual autobiography, highlighting aspects of their relationship with God from early childhood until the present. This will give me a clearer picture of who they are as spiritual beings. Sometimes people are brand-new to faith, and know very little about the Church or the Bible, let alone a disciplined prayer life. In that case the first priority is to get them integrated into the rhythm of a parish, and at times prepare them for baptism.

With beginners I usually start by grounding them intellectually, having them read books that we can discuss. For understanding church life I use *Liturgy for Living*, by Charles P. Price and Louis Weil. For basic issues in Christian doctrine I find C. S. Lewis' *Mere Christianity* the most helpful. Once they have a good grasp of the basic issues of the Christian life, I will have them read Richard Foster's *Celebration of Discipline*, which is an excellent introduction to a life of prayer. Then I will map out a regimen of prayer and study for them to follow, and we will continue to meet about once a month for ongoing discussion.

If I discover the person is already well grounded in Christian basics, and if we agree to continue to work together, I will ask him or her to do an inventory of oblation before we meet again in two weeks. Oblation means offering. In the liturgy, the oblation takes place when the offering of money and bread and wine is raised before the altar. In personal prayer, oblation is the offering of self to God. An inventory of oblation takes place in six parts. I ask people to prayerfully hold before God six different aspects of their being: their emotions, will, intellect, imagination, relationships, and work. A time of prayer is set aside for each of these six aspects. For example, when it's time to offer their emotions, I will ask them to quiet themselves before God, and ask the Holy Spirit to show them in their emotional life, what they were giving to God, and what they were holding back.

There is no way to predict what will happen in these times of oblation. Some people may discover that it's easy for them to give God happy feelings of praise and thanks and joy, but that they cling to anger, jealousy, and fear. Others may discover the very opposite. I always ask my directees to keep prayer journals, and record what they experience every time they pray. The journal will be an objective point of reference for our discussions. After I meet with people a third or fourth time, and go through their experiences with the prayer of oblation, I will have a fairly accurate picture of where they are in the "Circle of Piety" (page 57). Then I will design a course of study and prayer that will affirm where they are and help them to grow in their own unique spirituality. We will continue to meet about once a month. Once they are securely well informed about their own particular piety, I will help them to explore other areas of the Circle of Piety.

I almost never plan anything for an ongoing session. My task is to respond to whatever has happened in their relationship with God during the time since we last met. When I offer a new direction, I take great care not to project any expectations, because nothing should interfere with what happens between these people and God. There are times when God is acting so powerfully in people's lives that it is as if they were caught up and swept along in a great and mighty river. My job then is to simply calm their fears, assure them that the intensity will not last forever, and let them know that they are not crazy or isolated, because many other Christians have had the same experiences. Basically, I become like a raft they can float on, keeping their head above water, enabling them to eventually get their bearings and set a new course.

There are times when the issues that prayer leads people to deal with are so overwhelming, they feel caught up in a terrifying storm, surrounded by awesome, crashing waves. Sometimes they will blame me for putting them in that particular predicament. In any case, it is then my responsibility as spiritual director to lead them through it. They may also need the help of a psychotherapist, or we may need to explore different kinds of spiritual healing. In my experience, no one has ever wanted to go back. They have always wanted to work through it. Because even in the midst of the terror, they have been able to recognize the assuring voice of God, beckoning them on in hope to the place of peace and joy and love.

Sometimes a person in spiritual direction will go through a crisis of faith. When Father William was a young monk he began to study intellectual history He was deeply impressed by how honest and sincere people rejected the gospel of Jesus Christ. He began to think that the claims of Christianity were not intellectually convincing. Since people with minds so much better than his own dismissed the gospel, William asked himself, "How can I have faith?" Soon he felt that he no longer did believe. For him it became not just a question of leaving the monastery, but of whether he would remain a Christian. He took his anguish to his spiritual director, Father Sean.

The learned old monk replied, "William, you do believe. But your faith isn't in your mind, it's in your heart, in your love, in your will. Faith is the gift of God. It is not the result of sincere intellectual study. Theology and apologetics only remove obstacles to faith; they never prove faith. If you simply offer to God your life patterned on Jesus, you will see your faith."

William spent the most difficult two months of his life struggling to follow Father Sean's advice. Finally, in a gradual movement of grace, it happened. He realized that faith is an inward illumination by God of something so good, the heart says, "Yes, I want it." So ultimately faith is an act of the will. It is beyond our mind's ability to express it, but it may be revealed by symbols such as the Eucharist, or the life of faith of another. During his time of crisis, William passed through his doubt relying solely on Father Sean's faith that he had faith.

There are times in the Christian life when nothing happens. Prayer becomes the same old boring, or even loathsome, routine. The waters have not become just still, but stagnant and torpid. This is what the Desert Fathers and Mothers called *accidie,* the overpowering desire to just chuck the whole thing. I mean, who needs God anyway? Father William describes it as being "entombed, lying alive in a coffin." Since I know even if my directees don't, that their stagnation is a temporary condition, in situations like this my task is to become more active. Sometimes the best approach is to back off the discipline and become more relaxed. I will often have people read novels, usually those by Christians like Dostoyevski, Tolkien, Flannery O'Connor, or Walker Percy, during time they would normally be praying. With other people, what they need is an entirely new approach to prayer. If their piety is emotional and sensual, I will have them move to an entirely different quadrant of the Circle of Piety, perhaps by having them read someone astringently mystical and intellectual such as Simone Weil, or by developing use of the Jesus Prayer.

In ongoing relationships, the quality often changes from teacher and student into more of a friendship. Instead of exploring and discovering new things, it becomes rather a place for guidance, discernment, and accountability. It is always important to remember that spiritual direction is a temporary relationship. Sometimes there are personality conflicts that become too disruptive. For example, I find it practically impossible to work with women toward whom I'm sexually attracted. My confessor, says I should never work with a woman under the age of eighty. Because of past experience I almost always decline to work with these women and refer them to someone else.

I am also reluctant to work with people in my own parish, because I see them in so many different settings under so many different roles that it makes the task of spiritual direction very confusing. In the teacher/student kind of relationship, working with friends is also extremely difficult because too much familiarity blurs the focus. I actually do my best work with people I don't see except for spiritual direction. But even the closest, most fruitful relationships have a natural life span. I feel I can teach another everything I know about prayer in about a year and a half. When we both recognize this, it is best for the relationship to end, for the person to be on his or her own with God, or to begin working with someone else who can teach new things.

SEEKING SPIRITUAL DIRECTION

As I have already indicated, finding a spiritual director may be very difficult. Begin by asking your minister or priest about it. Even if he or she may not be willing or able to perform it with you, perhaps someone else can be recommended. Finding a spiritual friend is far easier. The best way to go about it is to join a church or Christian fellowship group, and simply get to know people in a personal way. Then pray. Ask God to lead you to a person or group of people who will open up the reality of *koinonia* for you. He will.

Spiritual direction is not a necessity in the Christian

life. It is a gift, a means of grace with biblical and historical precedent, which may be utilized to help orient a life from self toward God. For me, as for many others, living as a Christian in a society that is essentially ungodly is extremely difficult. I need all the help I can get. I'm sure I would survive as a person of faith without spiritual friends, but my life would then be greatly impoverished.

5

THE VARIETY OF PRAYER

*T*HOMAS MERTON SAID, "If you want a life of prayer, the way to get it is by praying." So how does one begin a life of prayer? Dom Chapman said it is best to pray as you can, not as you can't. Begin with what you know about prayer and use that as the basis for beginning a relationship with God.

A few years ago I prepared a group of young teenagers for confirmation. Near the end of our course I met with them individually to talk about developing a life of prayer. One of the girls came from an unchurched family. When I asked her if she ever prayed, she said yes, and described how she prayed every morning when she got up and every evening before she went to bed. I was very impressed both by the scope and quality of her devotion. When I asked her who taught her to pray like that, she said she learned from watching "The Little House on the Prairie" on television. She took Laura as her confirmation name.

Everybody knows at least something about prayer, even if it is just knowing the Lord's Prayer by heart. The Lord's Prayer is an excellent place to start. Set aside fifteen minutes in a day, and offer those familiar words to God, not mechanically, but savoring them, sitting before God with every phrase. Ask the Lord to come to you, revealing himself to you in each phrase, helping you to understand what the words mean. *Our Father* . . . "Are you my Father? Do you love me as a parent loves a child? Show me your love; let me enter it." *Who art in heaven* . . . "What is heaven? Where is it? Can I enter heaven? Can I ever be there with you? Show me heaven; reveal it to me; help me to understand." *Hallowed be thy name* . . . "What is your name? Reveal it to me. What does it mean to make it holy? Can I ever be holy? Send your Spirit to me; transform me into holiness." Go through the prayer like that, asking questions, offering yourself to God through those words, entering into the prayer itself. Don't move along too quickly. Don't be afraid to become still in each phrase, to enter a place of solitude with it, and to wait there for God.

Other famous prayers may be used in the same way, such as the Prayer attributed to St. Francis, which begins, *Lord, make me an instrument of your peace* . . . For people who come from liturgical traditions, the prayer services may be used this way for personal devotion. After I had been renewed in faith for a few months, I happened to pick up Barbara's *Book of Common Prayer*. As I read through the Morning Prayer liturgy for the first time, I was swept into God's presence. All the inchoate feelings and longings that had been bottled up inside me were there on the printed page, expressed with a beauty and clarity far beyond my ability. I was particularly moved by the General Confession.

We have erred, and strayed from thy ways like lost sheep. We have followed too much the de-

vices and desires of our own hearts. We have left
undone those things which we ought to have
done; And we have done those things which we
ought not to have done; And there is no health
within us. Restore thou them that are penitent;
According to thy promises declared unto mankind in Christ Jesus our Lord. And grant, O most
merciful Father, for his sake; That we may live
a godly, righteous, and sober life.

Of course, these prayers can become rote. But if
they are prayed with attention and care, relishing their
meaning, invoking the Lord through them, using
them to enter the place of solitude before him, they
can become the vehicle for beginning a redemptive
relationship with God. The power of these prayers is
not just in the beauty and appropriateness of the language. It is also found in the fact that these very words
have been prayed by Christians for centuries, as well
as today by Christians on every continent, all across
our planet. When we pray them now, in a mystery
beyond our ken, we are drawn into the communion
of saints, the body of Christ.

Where else can one turn to begin a relationship with
God? Well, every human being dreams. Psychologists
disagree on the function and meaning of dreams, but
there is wide consensus that dreams are a symbolic,
imaginative processing of repressed emotions bottled
up in the unconscious. Is it possible that God may
speak to us through our dreams? There is certainly
biblical precedent. God revealed his will to the prophets Nathan and Daniel in their dreams, and gave the
patriarch Joseph the ability to see his will in the

dreams of others. Yet the strange symbols that represented his revelation demanded a specific gift of spiritual discernment for correct interpretation.

Even though we all dream, most of us are cut off from our dream life, and only infrequently remember our dreams. It takes a special effort to remember. When I wake up in the morning, I will concentrate in order to keep dreams in my conscious mind, and if one is particularly striking, I will write it down in my journal. Why do I bother? Because I think at times God speaks to me through my dreams. To correctly interpret spiritual messages in dreams takes a special skill and discernment. I sometimes discuss dreams with my spiritual friends, and frequently use dream material in the spiritual direction I do with others. If you intend to pursue this spiritual path, always consult with someone whose ability you trust.

There is another avenue to an active prayer life, which, although accessible to anyone, also requires the guidance of a discerning and skilled spiritual director. This is opening one's imagination to the presence of God. It is an ancient practice of prayer, first proposed by the great anti-Gnostic theologian Irenaeus (c. 130–c. 200). Irenaeus called Christians to the "imitation of Christ" by identifying and embracing Jesus' Passion in their imagination. He felt that through this type of prayer, God would transform the believer's mind into the mind of Christ, in the hope that he or she would be empowered to overcome sin, and live a Christ-like life.

This discipline was taken up centuries later by Ignatius Loyola and Francis de Sales, discussed in the previous chapter. Their method begins with the selection of a story from one of the Gospels, and then meditating on it by re-creating it in your imagination. The goal is to use your imagination to project your consciousness into the scene itself. Take, for example, the story from Mark 4 of Jesus stilling the storm. After quieting yourself, imagine what it would have been like to have been there. What did the boat look like? How were the disciples and Jesus dressed? Who was sitting where in the boat? Where were you sitting? Begin then to engage the rest of your senses. Feel the hard wood of the gunwale digging into your back. Smell the sharp odor of fish. Hear the rush of the wind and waves. Then, once the scene is set with you there, let the story unfold through free association, letting your mind flow. Before you draw yourself out of the scene, imagine that Jesus turns to you and speaks. What does he say?

This kind of prayer may seem ridiculous to you. Many people have a difficult time believing that God could act through something so obviously a projection of their own psyche. They argue that any revelation arising from imaginative free association would have to be the extension of wish fulfillment. If you feel that way, it's okay. Don't pursue it. Many great writers on prayer avoided the imagination at all costs. The fourteenth-century monk, Gregory of Sinai, wrote that praying with the imagination led one to become a "fantasist instead of a hesychasist." Teresa of Avila felt that the imagination led to the spirit becoming overrun with "little lizards" of doubt.

But when I have worked with others in spiritual direction, I have found that for some people this kind of prayer has been the key to opening a rich intimacy with God. I have seen amazing results from it. But again let me stress that this kind of prayer requires the guidance of a skilled spiritual director, and should only be practiced if you are working with someone whose judgment and discernment you trust. The reason is obvious. With imaginative prayer, even the most mature Christians need objective criticism to help separate their own projections from spiritual reality.

CENTERING PRAYER

The goal of a life of prayer is *koinonia*, an intimate relationship with God. In developing a life of prayer that will lead to deep intimacy with God, everyone needs to develop a kind of centering prayer, a focusing of concentration, a letting go of self, a calming, quieting process of shutting out the superficial, in order to fully enter the presence of God. In John 17, Jesus prays to God the Father for us, asking that we be drawn into the life of the Trinity, "one as we are one." Centering prayer is what takes us to that place in our being where God will meet us.

In that place of prayer, God himself will show us our true identity. It is ours already. It is God's gift to us in Jesus Christ. It is our inheritance through faith in Jesus Christ and through baptism. We will take complete possession of it at our resurrection. Through centering prayer we enter into it *right now*. Thomas Merton wrote, "We already have everything, but we don't know it, and we don't experience it. Everything has been given to us in Christ. All we need to do is experience what we already possess."

There are several things that prevent us from centering. One is our emotional need to dominate every relationship, even a relationship with God. The need to be in control does not allow us to let go of ourselves, and consequently, we are always holding something back. As we fill the stillness with our own jabberings, we are unable to hear the voice of God.

Another problem is our tendency to project our experiences in human relationships onto God. Every one of us has had to deal with authority figures, parents, teachers, clergy, nuns, and others who have unconsciously shaped the way we view God. It is very difficult for someone who received affirmation from her father only when she lived up to a certain standard to enter into God's unconditional love. It is very difficult for someone who grew up in a broken home to trust that God will always be there, and never abandon her. It is very difficult for someone who was beaten in primary school by a sadistic, bitter nun to believe that God loves him. All of these and other projections must be stripped away by centering prayer.

Sometimes the theology or emotional ethos of the church a person grew up in will make centering prayer almost impossible. A particular theology or piety can prevent a person from entering into deep intimacy with God. There is a brand of American Protestantism called Dispensationalism whose adherents believe that God related to humanity in different ways during different historical dispensations or divinely appointed ages. For example, gifts of the Spirit like speaking in tongues were intended by God for the "Apostolic Dispensation" only. Since we are now living in the "Church Dispensation," speaking in tongues is considered by them to be a violation of God's will and thus the work of Satan. Perhaps speaking in tongues could have been the very vehicle of centering prayer that would have led a Dispensationalist into a deeper fellowship with the Lord. Centering prayer demands we give up all our prejudices, even our religious ones, and be totally open to God.

Formalism, the ease with which we slip into form instead of substance, may also make centering prayer very hard. I often go to a restaurant in the East Village of New York called Around the Clock Café. Once when I was there, I was sitting near a young punk couple. The man was flipping through a magazine while the woman prattled away nonstop. Whenever she paused, he would say "Uh huh" without even looking up, and she would continue on. How often, I thought, is my prayer just like that? How often have I rushed through the familiar words without any attention, completely absorbed in myself? Centering prayer is the very opposite. It is about intimacy. Through it I become fully, totally aware of who I am in that very moment, and in the same moment I become fully, totally aware of the life-giving, joyous love of God.

Centering prayer became central to the discipline of the Desert Fathers and Mothers. They sought to embody in their lives St. Paul's dictum, "Pray without ceasing." Based on two prayers recorded in the Gospels, that of the blind beggar Bartimaeus in Mark 10, and that of the repentant publican in Luke 18, some of the Desert Fathers developed a special prayer. Abba Macarius the Great (c. 300–c. 390) taught his followers to use few words when they prayed, such as, "Lord, according to your will, have pity on me." This eventually evolved into what is called the "Jesus Prayer." For support he quoted the Apostle Paul in 1 Corinthians 14:19, *I would rather speak five intelligible words, for the benefit of others as well as myself, than thousands of words in the language of ecstasy*. In Greek (as in Russian), the Jesus Prayer has five words!

One of the Fathers of the Egyptian desert, Abba Isaac (c. 400), used the formula "O God, come to my assistance. O Lord, make haste to help me." He felt that this prayer led to a place beyond the senses, without any visual image, thought, or words. Only at that place would there be a pure giving of self to God. Medieval champions of the Jesus Prayer also stressed the movement beyond the senses. William of St. Thierry, a 12th century Cistercian monk, felt that praying with images was idolatry, because God was found only in the purity of relationship in his image stamped in every human being. In the modern era the Jesus Prayer shaped the piety of the Eastern Orthodox Church. It has also passed into popular culture through novels such as J. D. Salinger's *Franny and Zooey*.

In his book *Centering Prayer*, the Trappist monk Basil Pennington writes in detail about practicing the Jesus Prayer. Its basic form is "Lord Jesus Christ, have mercy on me a sinner." It is tied to the rhythm of breathing, saying the first phrase while inhaling and the second while exhaling. Many of its practitioners, including Father William, focus the prayer even further, reducing it to the *name*: "Jesus." Using the fourteenth-century English classic *The Cloud of Unknowing* as his authority, Pennington says that any words that are personally meaningful, such as "love" or "joy" or "let go," may be used. I think that is a serious mistake. The purpose of the prayer is to enter the life of the Trinity. That is done by invoking Jesus, the Great High Priest himself, and entering his prayer. There is no other way into the deepest intimacy with God. If the prayer does not focus on God the Son, it will be off-center.

Pennington bases the discipline on three helpful rules. The first is to use the prayer to quiet the self. The motive of the prayer is love, a loving assent to the reality of God. It allows the self to be filled with the desire to be with him, to be completely open to him, to rest in his presence. Once the self is in God's presence, the second rule is to concentrate totally on him. The third rule is to use the prayer to fight off distractions. It is very common to discover one's concentration has drifted away from the Lord. When this happens, the prayer can be used to nudge the self back into intimacy.

Teresa of Avila writes about two rivers of consciousness inside us. One flows into God, the other into some sort of activity. It is analogous to being at a cocktail party, engrossed in conversation with one person, while around us flows all kinds of noise, activity, and chatter. Through the Jesus Prayer, we can stay focused on God, engrossed in God, while our thoughts, feelings, and images flow on all around us. Or perhaps, in response to the Spirit, using the Jesus Prayer, our thoughts, feelings, and images may be given to God. The point of the prayer is to give the self entirely to the present reality of God.

How much time should be given to the Jesus

Prayer? The anonymous author of the *Way of the Pilgrim* offered the prayer twenty-five thousand times a day. He learned to offer the prayer constantly, even while he was engaged in work or conversation. Some of the Desert Fathers and Mothers did the same, praying the prayer all day long as they wove baskets, plaited ropes, and carried out other duties. Father William offers the prayer for nearly two hours every morning.

But what about us, who have families, jobs, and other responsibilities? I think it is appropriate to set aside half an hour every day. Begin with reading a passage from the Bible in order to move the mind away from the pressing demands of the moment toward God. Settle yourself in a comfortable position and begin to offer the prayer. Simply give yourself over to it. You cannot control what will happen, it cannot be forced, so just open yourself in trust to the Lord. It is a passing into another state of consciousness, from self-reflection into pure consciousness. After about twenty minutes, bring yourself out of it by reading a Psalm or reciting the Lord's Prayer.

During my first year as a priest at St. Bartholomew's Church in New York City, a woman in the parish named Merle Wahler offered to teach a course in centering prayer. Although it was to meet early on Wednesday mornings, I decided to take it, because at the time I didn't know anything about centering prayer, and she was a person whose piety I respected. The course was over eight weeks. As about half a dozen of us gathered in the dreary mortuary chapel in the church's basement, Merle very skillfully prepared us for centering prayer.

The way she talked about intimacy with God created great desire for him. She took us through the thoughts on prayer of great Christian saints, from the Desert Fathers and Bernard of Clairvaux to Julian of Norwich and Teresa of Avilia. Then, during the final session, using a guided meditation, she took us to the place of centering prayer. For me it was a route I'd never taken before, and on the way I was eager in anticipation. When we arrived at the place, the place where God would meet us, I was surprised to discover it was a place I went all the time, several times a day. Yet my vehicle for going there was different from the prayer discipline Merle taught. I went there by speaking in tongues.

For those who are unfamiliar with it, speaking in tongues often seems to be something fearsomely strange. It certainly was for me when I first encountered it in the Madison Prayer and Praise Community. That fellowship was charismatic, which meant that speaking in tongues, prophecies, healing prayer, and prayer for the use of spiritual gifts were common. Speaking in tongues was considered to be the ultimate sign of God's blessing. Among members of the community there was an unspoken elitism about having the gift of tongues. Yet the prospect made me very nervous. It seemed too weird to me. In the relationship I had with God, I didn't have to go off into spiritual space to encounter him; the Lord Jesus Christ came to me where I was. For me, speaking in tongues represented losing control, of again being lost in some psychotic or spiritual space.

When I shared my concerns with my spiritual friend Bob Salinger, he suggested that I talk with Jim Egan, a Jesuit attached to the University Catholic Center, who had had similar reservations. I had never had much time for Catholics before, and I went not prepared to receive advice, but to do battle. I began our conversation by telling him that the Cult of the Virgin had grown out of popular worship of the Mother Goddess by Mediterranean peoples. Jim only smiled and said I was probably right. He was so gracious, I was totally disarmed. When we talked of "glossalalia," or speaking in tongues, he convinced me that it was a gift over which the recipient exercised complete control. It was a prayer language that bypassed the intellect, so that a person could communicate directly with God, spirit to Spirit, person to Person.

I decided I would ask God for the gift, but privately. It remained too volatile an issue for me to explore in public. Jim told me that I should ask God for the gift of tongues in the name of Jesus Christ, and then just start using it. I might have to make myself utter a few sounds to get it going. So on my next day off, I went up to my bedroom, got down on my knees, and asked God to give me the gift of tongues. I remembered that Jim had said that I had to will to use it, so I forced myself to utter a few guttural sounds. That was it. All that anxiety for a moment of gibberish. I felt foolish, but decided to try it again the next day. The same thing happened. But on the third day, I again prayed my request, opened my mouth, and had an entire language at my disposal.

From that moment it has remained central to my devotional life. Although I don't know exactly what the words I'm offering mean, I do have the sense that it's a language. When I have prayed aloud, there are certain words that I recognize time and again. Now, I don't make a big deal about the gift of tongues. I have only prayed aloud in public two or three times, and regretted it each time. Many people whom I've worked closely with don't even know I have the gift. The reason I'm quiet about it is that I've seen how divisive it can be in Christian community. I know some Christians for whom speaking in tongues is so important, it becomes idolatrous. My sense is that they're worshiping the gift of tongues rather than God.

Yet for me, it is the most precious gift I've received from the Lord. When I offer it to him, regardless of where I am, or whom I'm with, or what I'm doing, I am drawn immediately into his blessed presence. Sometimes, in the quiet of my own spirit, I pray in tongues three dozen times a day: while riding the subway, or walking along New York's teeming streets; while listening to a derelict's woes or the strife of a couple during marriage counseling; when I'm sad or anxious or depressed and simply need his hopeful, comforting touch; when I'm so happy or fulfilled, I'm bursting with praise and thanksgiving and want to share my joy with him.

When I work with someone in spiritual direction, I will always have them use some sort of centering prayer. The Jesus Prayer is, of course, open to everyone. Speaking in tongues is a spiritual gift which must be asked for and received from God. Not everyone is called to it. I know others who pray the Rosary for centering, and others who use icons to focus their attention on the presence of the Lord. Everyone needs to explore to discover what is best in his or her own unique relationship with God.

THE COMMUNION OF SAINTS

In beginning a disciplined life of prayer it is important to be aware of the communion of saints. When I attended Fuller Theological Seminary in Pasadena, California, I was sponsored by the Congregational Foundation for Theological Studies. Once or twice a year, the Foundation would bring Congregational seminarians together from all over the country in order for us to get to know each other, and to teach us about Congregational polity and history. In the spring of 1974, such a conference was held at a Benedictine convent outside of Madison, Wisconsin. After the conference ended, I had a free afternoon before heading back to California. I decided to go into Madison, which had been my home for seven years, and visit Father Jim Egan at the University Catholic Center. He greeted me with his usual warm grace, but said that in ten minutes he had to celebrate the five-o'clock mass. He asked if I would be willing to read the lesson. During the mass he introduced me simply as a seminarian from the West Coast.

After it was over, a young man approached me and said he was contemplating seminary himself and wanted to talk. We sat outside the Catholic Center, right on State Street, and talked for about half an hour before he discovered I was Protestant and married. It didn't faze him in the slightest. When it was time for me to leave, he grabbed my hand and said, "Let's pray the 'Our Father' together." As we sat there praying the Lord's Prayer, in a place where not too many years before I had bought and sold drugs and had been involved in antiwar rioting, I felt quietly drawn into the unity of the Church. Along with this Roman Catholic young man, I became conscious of a chorus of prayer, linking not only Christians throughout the world, but Christians right across history. Every Christian who ever lived prayed that same prayer, and as we said the familiar words, I felt our voices mingle with millions of others. For the first time I understood what the word *catholic* meant.

In our individualistic society it is very easy to never look beyond ourselves, our parish, our denomination, or our country. Yet one of the great mysteries of Christian faith is that there is an invisible unity binding together all Christians, from Jesuits in Rome to Pentecostals in the shantytowns of urban Brazil, from primitives in Irian Jaya to Park Avenue matrons, and every Christian who ever lived. We are in living communion with anchorites who lived in the Egyptian desert, with Irish monks and nuns who faced the terror of the pagan Vikings, with the men and women who built the great cathedrals, with Japanese and Ugandan martyrs.

The same God who gave the promise of salvation to Abraham, centuries later warmed the heart of John Wesley. The same God who confronted the Apostle Paul on the Damascus Road, today fills Mother Teresa of Calcutta with compassion for the derelict. The same God who in the fourteenth century drew Julian of Norwich into ecstatic visions, today gives courage to Archbishop Tutu in South Africa. Our unity is the living presence of Jesus Christ. As we are made alive in the Spirit today, we are entering a relationship with the same Lord who blessed those who went before us.

Do Christian saints who lived centuries ago have

any role in the ongoing life of prayer for Christians today? Like the gift of tongues, the communion of saints is a divisive issue that has split the Church. In Roman Catholic and Eastern Orthodox piety there is an active sense of participation in the communion of saints, through the invocation of the Virgin Mary or particular saints to pray for the believer. However, the cult of the Virgin and the cult of the saints were among the first doctrines to be rejected by the Protestant Reformation. This Protestant rejection was based on two issues: the nature of salvation and the nature of authority.

Medieval piety taught that the greatest saints died with a surplus of merit. They could transfer this merit to the living, or to those in purgatory, to help them in their struggle for salvation. This whole scheme was seen by the Reformers, and Protestants down through history, as a mediation of redemption through human effort, or a salvation by works. Since this undercut the biblical principle of salvation by grace only through God's activity, it was unacceptable to the Protestants.

The Reformers also insisted that for Christians the sole authority for their practice of faith was the Bible. The more radical interpretation of this maintained that nothing not explicitly affirmed in the Bible was valid for the Church. Consequently, since there was nothing in the Scriptures about the prayers of the saints for the Church, the widespread piety of Catholics and the Orthodox was also unacceptable. Besides, since Christians have direct access to God in prayer, there should be no need to bother with the saints.

As a born-again believer, I accepted the Protestant

position on this issue. I began to expand my horizons during the summer of 1975, when I was in Israel to learn Hebrew. Barbara and I were living in the village of Ein Karem outside of Jerusalem. Two other groups of American Christians were staying in Ein Karem. One was a group of Roman Catholic priests and nuns, and the other was a group of young men from the South who were under the leadership of a man called Ed Durst. Ed was a graduate of Dallas Theological Seminary, the home of Dispensationalism. The graduates of Dallas Seminary I'd met before had been even more reactionary and Fundamentalist than I was.

Ed Durst had gone on a long spiritual journey, become Roman Catholic, and was in the midst of founding a new religious order to work for peace and reconciliation in Jerusalem. Most of the young men with him were still Protestant, but were there to explore his vision. Ed and I had long conversations about what I perceived to be the heresies of Rome, especially the cult of the Virgin. His defense of the Virgin was based on the relationship thousands of believers had with her, that she was a living presence in the Church. Like Jim Egan, he was winsome and gracious, but I remained unconvinced.

Six years later, when I was serving at St. Bartholomew's Church, I found tremendous fulfillment in teaching and preaching. I felt that I became the person God created me to be in the act of giving myself over to the proclamation of his Word. I was most aware of the reality of God during and immediately following a sermon or class. Once, after I had preached a particularly poor sermon on a Wednesday evening in the chapel at St. Bartholomew's, I felt terrible. It was as if I'd let God down and I'd let myself down, not to mention the few dozen people who were there to worship. In my misery I knelt in one of the pews to pray. I felt an immediate loving presence, a personal presence in response to my prayer, as if I were enfolded in caring arms. Yet it wasn't the Lord. I know him so intimately that I knew it wasn't him.

It was Mary. She didn't tell me who she was or introduce herself; I just knew. It hasn't been easy to fit this experience into my evangelical theology. What it forced me to do was think seriously about the communion of saints. Almost all Christians agree that after death, the saints live in God as they await the resurrection. They join with us to worship when the community gathers for the sacraments. That is part of the meaning of the Transfiguration, when Jesus consulted with Moses and Elijah about his Passion. They are a living presence in the Church. So, I ask, if we don't hesitate to ask Christian friends to pray for us, why should there be a problem in asking the living saints to pray for us?

If this conflicts with your understanding of God's will, then ignore it. Millions upon millions of Christians have wonderful intimacy with God without ever asking Mary or one of the saints to pray for them. As for me, I have never invoked the prayers of any of the saints, nor do I intend to. Yet my study has led me to understand that there is biblical warrant for asking Mary's intervention with the Lord. For example, at the wedding of Cana, when the wine ran out, the servants approached Mary and asked her to intervene with Jesus.

Mary has been an ongoing presence in my life. Particularly at times when I am hurt or confused, she is there with a special tenderness and care. Yet she always seems to be pointing beyond herself to the Lord. As I meditate on the Magnificat in the first chapter of the Gospel of Luke, I am often filled with wonder. Mary is the complete human *yes* to God. I thank God for her. I love her.

DISCERNMENT

I am sure at this point some of my Protestant brethren are snorting, "Humph, discernment! Swanson could use some!" In the spiritual struggle of life, we must discern what impulses are coming to us from God, and what are coming to us from an alien spirit. As the Apostle John said in 1 John 4:1,

> Beloved, do not believe every spirit, but test the spirits to see whether they are of God, for many false prophets have gone out into the world.

When we have what seems to be a supernatural experience, we must first test to determine if it comes from God. If we determine it is of God, we must then decide how it relates to other valid experiences and objective revelations of God's will such as the Bible, in order to decide our course of action. Sometimes these choices are clear; at other times we are forced to act without a sense of certainty. Very often we must turn to another for guidance.

Humility makes discernment possible. If we are seeking discernment or discretion from someone, it is crucial to be totally open and honest. Holding back, either out of fear or pride, will hinder if not prevent a godly insight from occurring. But humility is equally important for the one offering discernment or discretion. It is the quality that will allow a person to seek God's will rather than his or her own. Humility prevents a person from imposing his or her insights on another. It is a humility that refuses to judge. In *The Sayings of the Desert Fathers*, it was said,

> A brother at Scetis committed a fault. A council was called to which Abba Moses was invited, but he refused to go to it. Then the priest sent someone to say to him, "Come, for everyone is waiting for you." So he got up and went. He took a leaking jug, filled it with water and carried it with him. The others came out to meet him and said to him, "What is this, Father?" The old man said to them, "My sins run out behind me, and I do not see them, and today I am coming to judge the errors of another." When they heard that they said no more to the brother but forgave him.

If there are what seem to be supernatural experiences that are not of God, what is their source? Foremost are the projections of our own psyche. This is especially a problem for highly sensual Christians, those who use their imaginations in prayer. Yet sometimes it's not an image, but a message that needs to be tested. There was a young man who was active in the Madison Prayer and Praise Community I will call Bill. Bill was a deeply devoted Christian, fearless in bearing witness to his faith. He once sat down in a restaurant in the middle of a rude, raucous motorcycle gang and in a winsome way began to tell them about Jesus. About every two or three months, Bill would come to the elders and say that the Lord had told him he was to quit his job at a bakery and work full-time as an evangelist. The Lord also said that in order for him to fulfill this ministry, the community was to pay him a salary.

How is such a "message from God" to be tested? It is a biblical principle that any call to ministry must be confirmed within the community of faith. If God is genuinely calling someone, it will be recognized and affirmed by others in the fellowship. In the case of Bill, the elders of the Madison Prayer and Praise Community did not confirm his call. God most definitely did not give the message Bill heard to anyone else. It was the sense of the elders that Bill had a terrific emotional need to be out front, to be the center of attention, and this desire became garbled in his own mind as a call from God. Discernment exists within the community, not only from those set aside for leadership, but between spiritual friends, within prayer groups, and if necessary, within the entire fellowship.

Another source of false "supernatural" experience comes out of attempts to rationalize and justify sinful behavior.

I know that I, too, often try to justify what I know to be wrong. This is why I believe it is so important to be in fellowship, because so often we can't trust our own judgment. It is crucial for us to seek humility. The humility to ask others for advice when we know we're on shaky moral ground, and the humility not to impose our own sense of morality on others.

Yet I think there are areas of moral certainty. For a man contemplating adultery, the Bible clearly and objectively states that adultery is a violation of God's intention. Such a man is, of course, free to choose how he would work out his relationship with this woman, as well as that with his wife, but in my mind to invoke God's blessing for it approached blasphemy. To supporters of racism and sexism, I feel equally certain. Their adherence to the letter of particular passages of Scripture is a denial of that of other passages and the spirit of the whole.

The third source of false supernatural experience comes from an alternative spiritual reality. In the biblical cosmology, there is an invisible realm populated by demonic and angelic beings. The Bible says that Satan himself can appear as an angel of light. We live in a rationalistic age that both scoffs at the notion of the devil and is at the same time obsessed with the occult in popular culture. For people of faith, the best advice comes from British apologist G. K. Chesterton, who said we can make two mistakes about the devil: the first is to deny he exists, and the second is to pay any attention to him.

It is often just as easy for a person of faith to attribute too much to Satan as it is to attribute too little. Demonology was prominent in the Madison Prayer and Praise Community. The prevailing ethos was that if a person behaved in a compulsive way, it wasn't due to neurotic complexes or human sinfulness, it was due to demonic oppression. When people were depressed or behaving in strange ways, it wasn't due to psychological disorders, it was due to demonic oppression. Prayers of exorcism were fairly frequent.

During this time I was close to a young man named Billy. He was subject to tremendous mood swings, and would sometimes act as if he were out of touch with reality. After thinking about the teaching I was hearing at the time, I became convinced that Billy was demon-oppressed. The prayer of exorcism was fairly simple. The first step was, in the name of Jesus, to command the demon to name itself. Demons cannot resist the power of the name of Jesus, and are forced to reveal their own names. Knowing the name of a demon gave one power over it, so the next step was, in the name of Jesus, to command the demon to leave the person being oppressed.

Since Billy wasn't a believer, and I didn't feel I could confront him directly, I decided on an ambush. I went to his apartment on the pretext of a social visit. After we'd chatted for a few minutes, I looked directly into his eyes and said in my firmest voice, "In the name of Jesus, I command you to name yourself!" A look of bewildered panic crossed his face before he uttered quietly, "Billy."

He was later diagnosed as being a degenerative schizophrenic, and was treated with success medically. I learned that what some Christians call demonic oppression is in reality mental illness.

In my own life at the time, I was troubled by behavior and thoughts that I had difficulty controlling. I began to wonder if I wasn't demon-oppressed. I had read a book called *Deliver Us from Evil*, by Don Basham. Basham was a Presbyterian minister, and the book was the story of how he had been led from normal parish work to a ministry of exorcism. The last chapter of the book gave instructions on how to exorcise yourself.

Barbara was in graduate school working on a master's degree in library science. She had to attend a conference at Notre Dame University, and I went with her. I dropped her off at the conference and drove back to the motel. Once in our room, I took out Basham's book and began to examine myself. The book said to command the demon to name itself by using the name of Jesus. I did, and not to my surprise, the answer came back, "Lust." I continued to follow the book's instructions, and in the name of Jesus commanded "Lust" to depart from me. Nothing happened. So I read a little further, and the book said that sometimes one has to help the demon along, by coughing for example. So I said, "Lust, in the name of Jesus, I command you to depart from me. Cough. Cough. Cough."

Still nothing happened. I tried it time and again, and each time nothing happened. After about twenty minutes I went on to a second problem. The name came quickly enough. It was "Sloth." "Sloth" wouldn't leave, either. After a while, it dawned on me that what some Christians call demon oppression is just plain old sin. It's too bad, but we just can't exorcize sin. Fortunately, it can be forgiven.

The greatest of the Desert Fathers was Antony of Egypt (c. 250–356), whose practice of world-denying, mystical prayer frequently took him far beyond his senses. His passionate struggles with and triumph over demons have been depicted by countless artists. Antony became the teacher and guide in prayer for dozens of other monks, impressing upon them the great need for the gift of spiritual discernment, which is the ability to see things the way God himself sees them.

The great spiritual writers talk about the dual nature of discernment. "Discernment of spirits" is a special divine gift of unique intuitive capacities. It is a spiritual gift (as is speaking in tongues), which must be prayed for. It cannot be nurtured or developed. It involves supernatural insight into another person's spiritual state, the ability to intuitively perceive the secrets of another person's heart, of which he or she may be unaware. Great saints were often considered great because of their gift of discernment. It is told that a group of young men went out from Alexandria into the desert to ask Antony whether they should become monks. The old man stopped them when they were still thirty yards from his cell and said, "Yes, yes. Become monks."

The second aspect of discernment is called "discretion." Discretion is a learned, rational capacity. It is available to and may be cultivated by all Christians. Richard of St. Victor (d. 1173) wrote that discretion was a deep insight into the reality of prayer which came through reading, listening, reasoning, and experiencing. His contemporary, Bernard of Clairvaux, felt that more than anything else, discretion demanded moderation, sobriety, and the avoidance of any extremes. It was blinded by both excessive zeal and mercy, by both excessive anger and tenderness.

It is important to constantly bear in mind that a vision of God leads to humility and obedience, while a vision of Satan leads to smugness and pride. The French saint Martin of Tours once rejected a vision of Jesus dressed as a nobleman. It is equally important to remember that a call from God does not perturb, or fill us with doubt and ambivalence. Even in the midst of trial and suffering, it leads to joy, calm, certainty, and assurance. John of the Cross wrote that a vision of God gives us perseverance in the face of instability.

When I remain wracked with doubt, I know I need to pray further. Yet when all else fails, I will often meditate on what Jesus would do if he were faced with a similar situation. There have been times, especially when a decision had to be made about a job offer, when I discovered God's will only after making the wrong choice. There remain times of moral uncertainty, when all the alternatives before me seem equally unclear. At times like that I fall back on Martin Luther's advice to sin boldly, in the knowledge that I am saved by grace alone, and that the God who is my Judge is also my Redeemer.

HEALING PRAYER

Barbara and I have a summer home in the Catskills, in a place called Twilight Park. For the first couple of years we were there, I regularly played tennis with a psychotherapist who had a tony practice on the Upper East Side of Manhattan. Our tennis skills were fairly even, and our matches were almost always close. Yet in the dozens of times we played, he never beat me a single time. One August afternoon, we were to play again. I had a bad cold and felt terrible, but decided to go ahead with the match. At one point, I was down five games to one, and I said to myself, "Well, it's finally going to happen. He's finally going to beat me."

I then won five games in a row. As I prepared to serve in the last game, when it was obvious to us both that I would win again, I couldn't help saying to him, "You know, Glen, there must be some deep unconscious reason why you can't beat me. I think you should talk to your analyst about it." He laughed, and said, "Oh, no. It's not unconscious at all. I know exactly what the problem is. I just can't do anything about it."

At times all of us have problems we simply don't know how to deal with. Healing is part of the Christian life. For many people God represents the possibility of healing when all else has failed. Many who otherwise ignore God will turn to him for healing, not only for physical ills, but also for crippling emotional and psychological problems. Whenever I teach about healing, I will ask how many in the room believe in healing prayer. Usually most of those present will raise their hands. Then I ask how many have actually experienced, or know someone who has experienced, healing through prayer. Fewer raise their hands. Finally I ask how many, when they are ill, seek God's healing before they take medication or go to a doctor. Very few raise their hands.

In the beginning a discipline of prayer, it is very important to have a clear understanding about the role of healing in the Christian life. Like all other ministries, Christian healing should take place in community. Beware of people who carry on healing ministries on their own. Several years ago, when he was rector of a parish in Tennessee, a friend of mine was involved in a healing team that traveled all over the South to conduct services. When he went on to serve as rector in other churches, he no longer participated in the ministry. The reason had to do with community. In Tennessee a large group of his parishioners called him to the ministry, and agreed to pray for it every day. At the other parishes, when the communities there didn't feel led to organize and support a healing ministry, he moved on to other things.

Some Christians teach that it is God's intention to miraculously heal every infirmity. I think they are derelict in doing this. In the first place, nowhere does the Bible indicate that this is God's purpose. Jesus' miraculous healings were never ends in themselves, but always part of a pattern of revelation about the Kingdom of God. Second, if it truly is God's intention to heal everyone who comes to him in prayer, what about those faithful people who seek yet fail to receive miraculous healing? Unfortunately, many of the unhealed believe that it is their own fault. They then believe there must be something wrong with them, perhaps a lack of faith or an unforgiven sin. As one who has had to pastorally deal with the consequences of this false teaching, I can only say it is utterly wrong.

Remember, the ultimate intention of prayer, and of the Christian life, is to be drawn into intimacy with God. We all live in a fallen world, where illness, suffering, and pain are part of the fabric of existence. What is the relationship between suffering, healing, and intimacy with God? Is it possible that without being the source of evil, God uses illness and pain to draw people into a deeper intimacy with him?

In his book *The Problem of Pain*, C. S. Lewis wrote

about two ways in which pain may lead to a closer relationship with God. The problem is that human beings are in rebellion against God. Instead of being humbly open before his sovereignty, instead of worshiping him, we have chosen to be self-determining, we have chosen to worship ourselves. However, pain destroys the feeling that everything is okay. Many if not most human beings won't begin to surrender to God as long as their lives are running smoothly. Pain is unmasked, unmitigated evil. It is impossible to ignore, and it shatters the illusion that what we have is our own and is enough for us. We won't turn to God if we have anyplace else to go. Pain affords us the opportunity to turn to him.

Several years ago, Robert Sorensen invited me to his house on East Seventy-second Street for lunch. He had attended some of the courses I'd taught at St. Bartholomew's Church. We discussed the possibility of together teaching a course on faith. Bob is an agnostic social psychologist, and the idea was to see what kind of dialectic we could create in examining faith issues from radically different perspectives. I was very excited by the prospect when suddenly a flu began to crash into me. I felt so woozy and out-of-whack that I decided I'd better get home as quickly as possible.

At the time we were living on Roosevelt Island, a residential community in the East River connected to Manhattan by an aerial tramway. The only problem was, that day the tram was down and island residents were being ferried by bus over the Fifty-ninth-Street Bridge. As I walked down Second Avenue, I became sicker and sicker. By the time I was waiting in line for the bus, I could hardly stand. The bus arrived and was crammed with people. I squeezed in and was held upright by the crush of other bodies. While the bus crossed over the bridge, waves of nausea swept over me. Now, I'm not one of these people who can politely throw up into a handkerchief. Nope, for me it's purely projectile vomiting. Just imagine what it would've been like on that bus if I'd started spewing vomit over everyone. But I didn't know whether I would be able not to.

Being a person of faith, I started to pray. Not just a wimpy "Assist me here, dear Lord." No, this was with passion. I threw my entire being into the prayer, "God, please! Please! Keep me from throwing up all over these people. Help me! Help me!" The first wave of nausea passed, but another came just as we entered Queens. I repeated my impassioned pleading, and again it passed. Finally we arrived on Roosevelt Island, and I stumbled from the bus to our apartment.

Once in the safe confines of our home, the flu asserted its power. I threw up a dozen times over the next six hours. Yet in the midst of that awful flu, the Lord was with me with a tenderness and care I've never experienced before or since. There is no question in my mind it was because of the passion of my prayer. Was I cured of the flu? No. When I've had the flu since then, was he there in the same way? No. But he was there that night, in the midst of, because of my suffering.

When a Christian is ill, or emotionally troubled, that misery should become part of his or her conversation with God in prayer. In God's plan, we may or may not be healed miraculously. How we are to pro-

187

ceed with God, whether to seek the laying on of hands, or simply offer ourselves before him, is a matter for discernment. When I was working as a conscientious objector at Madison General Hospital, I gave blood about every two weeks. My blood became the "control" for all the blood tests the hospital ran that particular day. Once, an hour after having given blood, a hematologist rushed up to tell me that either their computer was haywire or something was radically wrong with my blood calcium.

It turned out I had developed hyperparathyroidism, a disease that prevents the body from metabolizing calcium. Its symptoms are a gradual disintegration of the bones, and a collection of gravel in the bloodstream which will ultimately destroy the kidneys. Fortunately, mine had been discovered before any damage was done. It was to be treated surgically, by removing the parathyroid glands found in the neck.

At this time, Barbara and I were attending the charismatic prayer meeting that was held in the home of the university professor. During one of those meetings, the professor said the Lord told him there was someone present who needed healing in the neck. A woman raised her hand and said she had a sore throat. So the professor and others went to her, laid hands on her neck, and prayed for healing. Then a man said he had a cough. They laid hands on him, too. Then the professor said he thought it was someone else. Suddenly it hit. It was me! I was the one with the serious problem in my neck. I sheepishly raised my hand, identified the problem, and with great glee the group rushed over to me, put their hands on my neck, and prayed for my healing.

I was healed of hyperparathyroidism, but only after having surgery twice. Yet I felt the Lord sealed my healing when those people laid their hands on me. I went into both operations with total confidence and unshakable assurance. Yet the means of my healing, the means of the Lord's blessing, was the skill of the surgeons.

I have seen miraculous healing in the areas of emotional and psychological problems. This has been especially true through the sacrament of liturgical confession.

In the context of spiritual direction I've also used a prayer technique called the "healing of memories." I first encountered it through a book by Mathew and Dennis Linn called *Healing Life's Hurts*. It can be done with another person or alone. The technique involves re creating in the imagination a particularly painful memory, from early childhood to recent past. Once the emotional scene is set, the person invites Jesus into the memory and asks him to heal the pain. Using this prayer sometimes uncovers earlier memories that had been buried in the unconscious. I have seen crippling anxieties, bitterness, and self-hatred healed through this prayer.

Often the healing that takes place through prayer is gradual. The greatest single trauma of my life was the psychotic breakdown caused by LSD. The terror I went through then is something I hope never to experience again. The first year we were at Fuller, Barbara and I joined with a group of other couples for supper and prayer on Friday evenings. After one of these meetings, a woman I hardly knew came up to me and said, "It's going to be all right." Since I didn't think anything was wrong, I was a bit disturbed.

Later that night Barbara and I had a very intimate encounter, and we were able to resolve some issues that had been troubling our relationship for a long time. I was so excited that I couldn't sleep. At about two in the morning I got up out of bed and went into my office to read the Bible. The entire house was dark except for the light over my desk. Suddenly, without any anticipation, the most unspeakable demonic horror stood in the darkened doorway of my office. Intuitively, I realized it was personal and it wanted to destroy me. It demanded that I look at it. Every ounce of strength I had was needed to prevent myself from looking, because I knew if I did, I was finished. Its power was overwhelming.

I cried out to God for help and began to search desperately through the Bible for something to anchor me. Just as suddenly, I felt the Lord himself standing behind me. It was as if he put his arms around me, and slowly he began to draw me up. He took me to a place I hadn't been to in years. From that place of high consciousness I could see the entire spiritual universe spread out before us. He stood behind, with his arms around me, and declared that I belonged to him, and there was nothing, nothing that could harm me.

After a time I again was aware of being in my office. Slowly I made my way back to bed. Twice more that night the demonic horror returned, and each time I had to remember what had happened with the Lord. The final time that night, even in the midst of my terror, I realized that regardless of what skirmishes or battles remained in the future, a war, a personal aspect of a cosmic war, had been won, and I had been healed.

Healed of what? Although it was difficult for me to articulate then, I was healed of a terror that reached out for me from deep within my psyche. But the healing was to continue. In the autumn of 1977, when we were in Edinburgh, Barbara's mother, Helen Burden, became ill with cancer, and was given only weeks to live. We decided to fly to Maui in order to be with her. Since Barbara's father and brother-in-law are both doctors, it was decided to bring her mother home so she could spend her last days with her family. The following three weeks were very difficult as her mother's condition worsened. I felt so much tension, there was a constant tightness in my throat which made it difficult to swallow.

I had never been very impressed by Helen's Christianity, but when we had several conversations about afterlife, I was touched by the simple beauty of her faith. During her last week, she was hallucinating so much that she was almost totally out of touch. When the end approached, Barbara's father Al called us into her room. As we stood around her bed, I watched death come for her. Yet at the very moment she died, it was the Lord who was there. He gathered her in his arms. A stillness filled the room, as if heaven and earth had touched. We felt sorrow, yes, but in it and around it was joyous peace. Barbara led us in a prayer of thanksgiving.

On reflection, I realized that up until the moment of Helen Burden's passing, I had been terrified of death. It was a fear so deep in my psyche that many nights, in a panic, I would shake myself back into consciousness as I felt myself slipping into sleep. If I let myself go, I might never return. But as she died I looked death in the face and saw behind it the risen Lord Jesus Christ. I no longer feared death, but the healing was to continue.

Several years later, while working at St. Bartholomew's, I realized how much I lacked support for my own spiritual life. I met on a regular basis with my friend B. J. Weber, but I needed something more disciplined. I had met a Dominican priest named Daniel Morrissey, who was teaching spirituality at Union Seminary. He agreed to become my spiritual director.

Daniel insisted that the best theology was autobiography, and he continually forced me to discover the reality of God in the people and events of my own life, no matter how mundane they appeared on the surface. He believed that the real goal of a life of prayer is to discover our true identity in relationship with God. Our true identity is hidden in the heart of God, and God has a name for us that captures this uniqueness. At any given time, every individual is in the process of moving into or away from his or her identity. Spiritually everyone bears different, false names as they move toward or away from their identity in Christ.

One day when I was complaining about my work, Daniel suddenly said to me, "What is your name?" I tried to evade him, but he simply repeated the question. I was forced to look at myself in relationship to God in that moment. Almost involuntarily I responded, "Mistrust. My name is mistrust." Under the glare of his probing I was forced to admit that in spite of my not inconsiderable faith, in spite of my vocation, in spite my public posturing, deep down at the center of my being, I did not trust God.

About what? About my sanity. When I had been cast into psychic space many years before, and lived in the terror of never returning, I had basically cured myself. No doctors had been involved. No spiritual guides had been involved. I had put the cap on myself. I had kept it on myself. I had given God control over much, but not over that. That deep mistrust colored every aspect of my life. It made me unconsciously afraid of the future.

Daniel designed a course of prayer that enabled me to use this new self-knowledge and slowly pry off my clutching fingers and give up my emotional well-being to God. It is a course of prayer that has enabled me to move far more of my being into Jesus' promise of years before, "He belongs to me." It is a process that has enabled me to come closer to my true identity. The healing continues.

JUST BEGIN TO PRAY

So if you want a life of prayer, just begin praying. You don't need any special training or skill. Start with where you are right now, with what you know about prayer right now. If you're comfortable with probing the meaning of famous prayers like the Lord's Prayer, begin with it or another like it. As you gain confidence, move on into developing a centering prayer that makes sense for you. A whole new quality of existence awaits you in relationship with Jesus Christ. A discipline of prayer will open up your imagination and dreams. A discipline of prayer will lead to a growth in discernment and healing. But more than anything else, prayer will become the basis for discovering your true identity in intimacy with Jesus Christ. As Paul wrote in 2 Corinthians 5:17,

Therefore, if any one is in Christ, he is a new creation, the old has passed away, behold, the new has come.

6

THE LIFE OF PRAYER

STUDENTS TEND TO make heroes of certain individuals in their field. When I was at Fuller Seminary, the recognized ideal was Lloyd Ogilvie, a re-
nowned preacher who was the senior minister of the
Hollywood Presbyterian Church. When I was studying at New College, Edinburgh, there were a variety
of heroic figures, but the one who captured the attention of the evangelical students was a man named
Capt. Stephen Anderson. Retired from the British
Army, he was a Scottish laird who lived on a Highland
estate in Inverness-shire. He spent his time away from
the land working as an evangelist for the Kirk, the
Church of Scotland. Barbara and I became friends
with his daughter Katrina, and we were invited up to
their estate, Altna Criche, during our first winter in
Scotland.

I must admit that I went to meet the great man
with some skepticism. He certainly looked the part
of a Highland laird, coolly detached, tall, angular, gin-
ger-haired, with flinty blue eyes. He had been presented to me as one so much larger than life, I wanted
to see some flaws, a bit of humanity. After breakfast
our first morning, with about fourteen people

sprawled around the huge table, he took a big Bible, opened it to the tenth chapter of the Gospel of Mark, and read aloud.

Let the children come to me, do not hinder them; for to such belongs the Kingdom of God. Truly, I say to you, whoever does not receive the Kingdom of God with the faith of a child shall not enter it.

As he closed the big book, his youngest daughter Lucy, who was about seven, said to him, "Daddy, what is faith?" I smiled with inward delight as I said to myself, "Hmph, now I'll see what this guy is made of." Without hesitating, he responded, "Lucy, when we go to London, do you have to worry about packing your things?" And she said, "No, Mummy packs all my things." "Well, do you have to worry about getting to the station?" "No, Daddy," she laughed, "you always drive us to the station." "Well, do you ever have to worry about getting on the wrong train?" "Oh no, Daddy, you make sure we get on the right train." "Do you ever worry that we'll get off at the wrong stop?" "No, Daddy, you take care of all that!" "That, Lucy, darling, is faith."

Faith, which is itself a gift from God, is the key to the Christian life. The ultimate goal of a life of prayer is *koinonia*, entering into intimacy with God. For this *koinonia*, faith is far more important than great learning. Faith is far more important than passionate commitment to serve in ministry. For *koinonia*, faith is considerably more important than having ecstatic visions.

In his book, *The Ascent of Mt. Carmel*, John of the Cross described a series of visions and locutions of the Lord. He ended each by saying, "Far more important than this is faith." Once Father William was visited in his hermitage at New Melleray Abbey by a visionary mystic and her entourage. One of the woman's followers gushed to William, "She's seen the Lord this morning! Oh, I wish I could," to which he replied, "Didn't you go to mass this morning? Encountering the Lord in the bread and wine is far more miraculous than any vision."

For *koinonia*, faith is the only adequate means of relating to God. Faith is a simple openness and trust. Faith is not relying on ourselves, our own ability, our own achievement when it comes to our well-being. Faith is trusting that God will provide us with what we need, that God will give us the grace to live out our commitments and fulfill our responsibilities. Augustine of Hippo wrote centuries ago that God wants to give us a great gift. He wants to give us the gift of an intimate relationship with him. He wants us to enter the fullness of his life, the love, joy, and peace within the Trinity. But he can't give it to us because our hands are full. What are they full of? They're full of ourselves. We must put ourselves down and stand before God with empty hands before we can receive his gift. Even as we commit ourselves to enter a disciplined life of prayer, it is the faith of a child that enables us to offer empty hands to God.

DISCIPLINE IN PRAYER

From very early on in the life of the Church, men and women attempted to organize comprehensive, disciplined lives of prayer. The great fourth-century saints of the Egyptian and Syrian deserts lived out lives fully devoted to prayer. The first of the Desert Fathers to reflect systematically about prayer was Evagrius Ponticus (346–399). He was born in Pontus, received a theological education, and was eventually ordained a deacon. He served the great leaders of the Eastern Church, Basil of Caesarea and Gregory of Nazianzus, before settling in the Egyptian desert as a monk. Like most in the desert, his discipline of prayer was extremely mystical, because he, like they, felt that the two final things that prevented knowledge of God were passion and imagination.

For Evagrius, the life of prayer had three stages, which he called "prayer of the lips, the mind, and the heart." This discipline led first to *apatheia*, the freedom from passions, before moving on to knowledge of divine reason, and finally, entrée into the life of the Trinity.

Eastern monasticism was brought to the Latin-speaking West by John Cassian (360–435). Before he founded the monastery of St. Victor at Marseilles, he spent over a decade living with monks in the Egyptian desert. His great mentor was Evagrius Ponticus. He transformed Evagrius' three stages into "purgative, illuminative, and unitative prayer." Following the desert model, Cassian taught that successful prayer demanded *apatheia*, freedom from emotional demands, and disinterest in worldly things. However, he couldn't use the word *apatheia*, because Evagrius' teachings had already been scorned as heretical in the West by St. Jerome. So Cassian translated the Greek *apatheia* into the Latin phrase *puritas cordis*, or "purity of heart." Cassian's most lasting achievement was the organization of cenobitic monastic prayer around the recitation of the Psalter.

Centuries later, Francis of Assisi's great follower Bonaventure (1217–1274) picked up this triple way. Although a man of the highest intellectual attainments, he taught that a fool may have a deeper knowledge of the love of God than the greatest theologian in the Church. He believed that knowledge was of value only as it assisted a person to grow in intimacy with God. He, too, used the model of the three stages of prayer in seeking *koinonia*. First, "purgation" led to a clean conscience, then "illumination" established the promises of God in our mind, and finally the goal of "union with God," a pure relationship where one sees "nothing."

How should these three stages of prayer be understood by someone living in the twentieth century? The first stage has to do with repentance. The Greek word for repentance is *metanoia*, which literally means "to turn around." Using this model, any approach to God begins with the recognition that we are in rebellion against God, and that the first thing we must do is to "turn around" from serving self, and offer ourselves in repentance before him. So prayer would begin with confession, seeking God's forgiveness.

The second stage has to do with understanding. It particularly has to do with understanding biblical revelation, comprehending God's plan of redemption which took place in human history and culminated with the birth, death, and resurrection of Jesus of Nazareth. Using this three-part model, the second stage demands a discipline of study. This comes primarily

199

through reading and reflecting on Holy Scripture, but also through the study of other Christian writers. In prayer, it manifests itself in meditation on the works of God, offering him praise and thanksgiving for the wonder of "God become man, that we might enter the life of God."

The third stage is about *koinonia*, union or intimacy with God. As I've said several times, there is nothing mechanical about entering into this quality of intimacy. It can't be earned through disciplined asceticism, or esoteric mastery, or anything else. But it is what God wants for everyone, and the practice of centering prayer best prepares us to receive it.

Another kind of prayer discipline grew out of the lives of the Desert Fathers. There were two kinds of anchorites, those who withdrew to the desert. *Eremitical* monks were hermits who existed in almost total isolation. Some lived in remote, inaccessible places, such as at the top of rocky outcroppings. However, they were never completely cut off from society. Some of these "pillar saints," who had to lower baskets on a rope to stay supplied with food, depended on the generosity and service of others simply to remain alive. But most of the monks were *cenobitic*, which meant they lived in community. Although each monk had his own cell or cave, they would come together at appointed hours for prayer. This community prayer focused on the reading of Holy Scripture, and particularly the reciting of the Psalms.

Reform was brought to monastic life in the West by Benedict of Nursia (480–550). His "Rule" was intended not only to bring discipline to wandering monks, but also to change the quality of monastic prayer. The Rule contained the triple vows of stability, obedience, and humility. Stability meant spending one's entire life in a particular monastery. Obedience was to the abbot of that monastery and entailed chastity and poverty. Humility kept monks and nuns open to the grace of God.

Under the Benedictine Rule, the work of God (the *Opus Dei*) was the community's recitation of the divine office at the appointed hours. There was a clear division between prayer and work (*Ora et Labora*), in order to guarantee a good economic status for a large community. Eventually this resulted in many Benedictine monasteries becoming centers of tremendous wealth. Time not set aside for community worship and work was to be used for private prayer and personal devotions. This more balanced life, fed by the reading of Holy Scripture (especially the Psalms), has made Benedictine spirituality extremely sensual and emotional through the centuries.

The discipline of prayer that grew from these traditions described the life of prayer in four parts: *lectio, meditatio, oratio, contemplatio*. In the narrow sense *lectio* was the reading and hearing of Holy Scripture. It begins with the faith that it is the voice of God speaking through the Bible, and when we invoke the Holy Spirit, we may hear his voice speaking to us personally and intimately. In a broader sense, *lectio* means being open to the voice of God speaking in other areas: in the liturgies of the Church; in any proclamation of the Word, from sermons to personal witness; through the evocative power of art; through the beauty and majesty of Creation itself. *Lectio* means being sensitized to listen for the voice of God in all situations.

Meditatio involves internalizing the Word of God. It is the discipline of sitting prayerfully and reflectively, seeking to understand the truth of the gospel. In a certain sense, its goal is a movement from the intellectual to the emotional, so that what is known propositionally will become known existentially. It is the discipline of letting the Word of God become part of our being, shaping who we are.

The concept of memory became important in *meditatio*. It must always be kept in mind that while human beings live in time, and thus experience reality sequentially, God exists outside of time, in eternity. Whenever a person experiences the presence of God in his or her life, it is as if heaven and earth meet, the eternal breaking into the temporal. Consequently, when in prayer a person remembers and meditates on a particularly profound moment in his or her relationship with God, it is as if that past moment becomes a reality in the present. He or she will again enter into the eternal, timeless presence of the living God, through memory.

In the same way, but in a different context, this is what happens in the celebration of the Eucharist. The community gathers together to witness the acting out of the death and resurrection of Jesus Christ, and as the priest consecrates the bread and wine, it becomes the body and blood of the Lord. Christians have gathered together to celebrate this event in an unbroken stream of worship stretching all the way back to the Apostles in the Upper Room with Jesus himself. When we meditatively remember Jesus' death and resurrection, we are drawn into the collective memory of the Body of Christ. The experience of the eternal presence of the risen Lord that began on the first Easter morning becomes a present reality whenever and wherever the Eucharist is celebrated: at Alexandria in 300, at Rome in 700, at the monastery at Cluny in 1000, at Assisi in 1200, at Geneva in 1560, at Kampala in 1890, at Sao Paulo in 1950, at Jerusalem in 1987.

In the practice of the *Opus Dei*, monks following the Benedictine Rule felt *oratio* to be their community response to God in the liturgies of prayer. But in a wider understanding it is any discursive response in conversation with God. It would include presenting the stuff of our existence, our anxieties and hopes, our joys and sorrows, to God. *Oratio* involves seeking God's will when we're uncertain, seeking his comfort when we're hurt or afraid, giving him thanks and praise when we're fulfilled.

The fourth part of this approach to the life of prayer, *contemplatio*, or "contemplation," is the same as the unitative prayer, or union with God, which is the third stage in the first model. It is the prayer where our whole being says *yes* to God, when we are drawn into such intimacy with him that we enter our true identity. It cannot be earned, but is God's gift of grace to us in Jesus Christ.

Another model for the life of prayer has developed in evangelical Protestant circles in the twentieth century. I was first taught it by friends when I was studying at Fuller Seminary. It goes under the acronym ACTS, which stands for four parts of prayer: "adoration, confession, thanksgiving, and supplication." Adoration is the prayer of deep intimacy with God, analogous to "unitative" and "contemplative" prayer.

Confession, presenting our sins before the Lord in repentance, is the same as the "purgative" prayer in the first model. Thanksgiving and Supplication are both discursive forms of prayer, the former recognizing the Creator as the source of life and blessing, while the latter seeks his will and blessing in a personal way.

All three of these models of prayer attempt to present a comprehensive discipline, one that covers every aspect of our lives with God. So what are the components of a discipline of Christian prayer revealed in these models? First there is *repentance*, the recognition that we are in rebellion against God, followed by an offering of self to him. Second, there is *hearing the Word of God*, understanding that we need to be shaped by the objective power of the Word, through studying the Bible, hearing sermons, taking classes, and reading theology and devotional literature. In prayer we can sit with and meditate on the things we've learned, asking the Holy Spirit to use them to re-create us in God's image. The third element in these disciplines is *offering ourselves to God*, by simply sharing with him all the issues and concerns of our lives that are of immediate import. Finally there is the goal of *intimate personal union with God, koinonia*, which comes only through grace, only through his initiative.

I think that each of these models is equally valid for giving structure to the life of prayer. If it is true that we were created to be in intimate relationship with God, if it is true that through this relationship we may enter the fullest meaning of human existence, then a discipline of daily prayer should be our highest priority. Exactly what a person's rule of life will be is an individual matter, determined by his or her identity in Christ as well as particular circumstances. Over the years my rule has evolved as both my situation and I changed. Right now I have arrived at a discipline that I find necessary and enriching.

I get up every morning at 6:00 A.M. for prayer. Once I get settled in a comfortable chair, I start by reading two chapters from the Bible, one from the Old Testament and one from the New Testament. After some reflection on the passages, I begin to pray. There are seven parts of this morning prayer: centering, praise, thanksgiving, confession, oblation, petition, and intercession.

I center by praying in tongues, letting myself flow with the prayer until I feel deeply drawn into God's presence. During the time for praise I usually ask the Holy Spirit to let me understand the Scripture I've just read. If I'm able to hear God's voice there, praise for his redemptive activity, or for his power, majesty, and love, just seems to come naturally. Sometimes I focus on a particular attribute of God, such as his power or his wisdom or his peace, and let myself be drawn in awesome wonder.

Thanksgiving is more personal. I thank God for the sources of joy in my life: for the gift of faith, for the love of my family, for the companionship of my friends, for the meaning in my work, for the comfort of our home, for the excitement and stimulation of New York City, for the beauty of the Catskills. If I'm going through any difficulty, I try to give God thanks for it, thanking him in advance for his wisdom and strength to enable me to grow through it. With both praise and thanksgiving, I try to be still before God, letting my prayer arise naturally and spontaneously. As a consequence, at times I spend much time there, and at other times I pass through quickly.

Next I move on to repentance, beginning with confession. I use the categories of the "seven deadly sins" of Catholic piety: anger, lust, envy, greed, gluttony, sloth, and pride. Sometimes my selfishness in a particular area is conscious, but I've discovered that awareness of much of my sin is subconscious. So as I offer each category to God, I ask the Holy Spirit to reveal to me what my sin has been. For example, as I sit quietly with anger, sometimes the Spirit will lead me into little nooks and crannies of my being, and I'll discover resentments or irritation or bitterness I hadn't been conscious of. When I feel the Spirit has plumbed an area of sin, I'll ask the Lord to forgive me, to let me experience his forgiveness, and to give me the power to forgive those who have hurt me. There are times when I realize that God wants me to make some sort of intervention or restitution with certain individuals, and I then must ask him for the courage to follow through.

The second part of repentance is the prayer of oblation, of offering myself to God. I use categories for this as well. There are six areas that I give to God: my emotions, intellect, will, imagination, relationships, and work. With each category I will be still before the Lord, asking the Spirit to show me what I'm holding back from him. For example, with emotions, through the prayer I may realize that I'm harboring anger against someone, or that I'm smugly relishing a triumph at the expense of another. Or with my imagination, I may be brought to realize that my subconscious fantasies have been about controlling the lives of others, manipulating them to my own ends. Whatever the Holy Spirit brings before me I will consciously offer to God, asking him to help me give myself to him completely.

Over the years the Spirit has taught me to be brutally honest in examining myself, in the knowledge that God forgives me, loves me, and desires me to enter fully into his life. Christians who live out a life of penance become free, and enter into *apatheia*. B. J. Weber once told me, "When I become aware of my sin, I don't feel guilty. I feel sorrow." Antony of Egypt said, "I no longer fear God, but I love him. His love casts out fear."

Petition and intercession are different modes of prayer. Petition is praying for my particular needs, and intercession for the needs of others. There are times when I can't help myself, and still blindly demand that God give me what I want. In the past few weeks I have insisted, "Okay Lord, you be sure this loan comes through, so I can rebuild the foundations under our house," or "Lord, I want no argument about this; you must heal her cancer!"

But over the years my attitude toward petition and intercession has been slowly transformed. Part of this is the realization that at times, when God gives what I insist on, it has disastrous consequences. Once several years ago, I decided that I wanted humility, and I was going to insist God give it to me. I told this to my confessor, and he said, "You be absolutely sure you really want humility before asking God for it. Because if you do, he's going to humiliate you." He was right; over the next months I went through a whole series of painful humiliations.

Out of this has grown the understanding that very often what I want for myself is not what God intends for me. God's desire for me is to be so filled with faith and trust in him that I can enjoy the deep intimacy he created me for. Very often my desires, even when they have a patina of "holiness," are for power or fame or success in a way that would make me self-reliant. I have grown to realize that God won't let me have some of the things I most desire, because if I had them, they would become idols separating me from him.

Jesus explicitly said in the Gospels that we were not to ask God for material things. (Matt. 6:33) What we are to ask for is intimacy with him. What we are to seek is the Kingdom of God, and simply trust that all our material needs will be met without our being anxious about them. The only place in the Gospels that could even remotely be construed as asking for material things is in the Lord's Prayer: "Give us this day our daily bread." But it is highly unlikely that "bread" in the prayer refers to material needs. Everyplace else where "bread" is used in the Gospels, its real meaning has to do with intimacy with God. After all, Jesus himself is "the Bread of Life" (John 6:35).

No, when we approach God with our petitions and intercessions, our goal should not be to argue God over to our side. Rather it should be to discover what God's will is in the particular issue. Augustine wrote, "We pray not in order to change God's will, but to change our will into conformity with his." It's not easy, when we're filled with desire or anxiety. It is much easier to adopt the attitude of the man who prayed, "Father, just this once, not thy will, but mine be done."

Our great example is Jesus himself in the Garden of Gethsemane the night before his death. As he contemplated the terror of his death, not just the excruciating emotional and physical torment of scourging, mocking, and crucifixion, but the horror of becoming an offering for humanity and receiving God's wrathful judgment against sin, his agony was so great that sweat fell from his face like great drops of blood. His earnest prayer was, "Father, if thou art willing, remove this cup from me; nevertheless not my will but thine be done" (Luke 22:42). In this prayer we enter into Jesus' humility, brokenness, and his trust in his Father.

"We pray not in order to change God's will, but to change our will into conformity with his." The goal of petition and intercession is to discover the mind of God, to be so united to him in the power of the Holy Spirit that we become of one mind. That is the saving event, when the Holy Spirit is so directing us that God's will becomes our will. Then, as Father William says, even when we enter the pit with no bottom, even as we enter unrelieved darkness, we can say, "I believe. Not my will, but yours be done."

I once asked Father William to define prayer. He waited two long minutes, in a kind of stunned silence, before saying, "Prayer is only a childlike expression of our needs and desires to our heavenly Father." So I take great care when it comes to petition and intercession. I don't try to deny any of my desires. If something is potentially obsessive, the best thing to do is give it to God. I want to bring my wants before the Lord as honestly as the Spirit enables me, but I know that what I should seek is God's will, not my own. Following William's instruction, every time I offer a petition, I release it before God, saying, "My Father knows."

When it comes to intercession, praying for the needs of others, I find I have to be selective. I will pray every day for my immediate family and my spiritual friends. I simply hold them up to God. Sometimes the Spirit will give insight or discernment into their special needs, sometimes not. Then I pray for those I know who are in critical need, and for each person who has an appointment with me that day. Then on particular days I will pray for specific groups. For example, on Sundays I pray for my greater family, on Mondays those people I have in spiritual direction, and on through the week.

You may think this is a three-hour routine, but if I can stay focused, it takes me about an hour. Of course, concentrating can be difficult. If I find my mind wandering, I pray in tongues until I'm drawn back into an awareness of the Lord's presence. I find that it is important to end the time of prayer with something that anchors me in the coming day, so I close by reading a Psalm.

I then wake up Barbara, and with coffee we have a brief devotional time together. We read a passage of Scripture, talk a little about it, share our schedules for the day, and then pray for each other. Sometimes our children, David and Katrina, join us. As a family we pray together every evening before the children go to bed. On Sunday evenings we have a special hour of sharing family tensions and praying together.

At some point in the middle of each day I set apart half an hour for contemplative prayer. I begin by reading and meditating on a Psalm, and then I give myself over to the Jesus Prayer. The only goal I have in mind is to enjoy being with the Lord. I never intend to focus on any issues, although sometimes he leads me in that direction. The prayer itself will take me beyond awareness of the words into an intimacy that is of supreme value. If my mind wanders, I repeat the prayer until it nudges me back to God.

That is my personal rule of life. Some days things happen to upset the pattern, but I will reassert it as soon as possible. Of course, it fits into my routine as a parish priest, which demands other times of prayer, during liturgies, counseling sessions, Bible studies, and with my colleagues. To someone who is just beginning the life of prayer, it may seem like an impossibly long time. But for me it seems too short. In the past I have set aside larger or shorter blocks of time each day. But this is the rule that works best for me now. The advice of Dom Chapman is sound: "Pray as you can, not as you can't." Figure out what you want from a life of prayer in the context of your life, design a discipline, and simply start doing it.

THE PRAYER OF THE HEART

There is a solitude, a place of quiet and calm, where human beings may meet God in the profoundest intimacy. It is the silence of faith in the presence of a mystery that a person cannot understand, yet believes. It is a place of such tranquility before God, one's whole being becomes like a still pool of water able to perfectly reflect the sun. It is "the prayer of the heart," which the great Desert Father Abba Arsenius (c. 360–c. 449) called *hesychasm*.

Many writers on the life of prayer couch *hesychasm* in terms of a quest for identity, an entrée into our authentic being. Just as a rose glorifies God by being a rose, we glorify God by becoming who we are in relationship to him. Basil Pennington tells the story of Rabbi Zuscha, who said, "When I get to heaven I won't be asked, 'Why weren't you Moses?' or, 'Why weren't you David?' but, 'Why weren't you Zuscha?'"

The prayer of the heart is not a return to anything, and it is not recapturing something that we intrinsically possess. *Hesychasm* is entering a new life which exists only in the resurrection of Jesus Christ. Father William says, "In Jesus Christ, there is a new 'I.' It is me united to him. It is me and Jesus together. We become one the way he and the Father are one."

In this union we enter into the very prayer of Jesus himself. Having gone to the center of our being, we discover our contingency and nothingness before God. As Thomas Merton wrote, "By accepting who we are, we pray. There is nothing more, and there could be nothing more. We have entered the fulness of God." In the mystery of the Holy Spirit, Jesus shares his life with us, transforming us into the person we are, the person God created us to be. We do not become God; we remain his creature. But in our own unique personhood we are drawn into the life of the Trinity. We see in this relationship that Jesus is praying, for us and for the world. We embrace his prayer, his life. We let him pray within us. By his grace we are fellow heirs, children of God. Our relationship with the Father and the Holy Spirit has become that of Jesus to the Father in the Holy Spirit.

The goal of *hesychasm* is not to acquire or deepen knowledge; it is a transforming experience of redemption. In the prayer of the heart, we become aware of who we are in terms of our sinfulness, our wanton selfishness and rebellion against our Creator. This awareness leads to *metanoia*, repentance in which we discover anew that we are beloved of God. Our true identity is always that we are a person who is loved by God, so loved that he paid the price of our redemption himself. Once we become aware of ourselves in this way, the prayer of the heart, *hesychasm*, contemplative prayer, is simply learning to rest in that love, to listen in silence.

Hesychasm may be understood as an attitude of prayer. It is much like oblation, because in it there is a surrender of ourselves to God. This surrender demands a willingness to descend into the depths of our own emptiness, trusting that the Word of God will come, trusting that God the Son will create in us a new being, and trusting that he will allow us to walk in it. The Christian spiritual writers speak of how difficult it is to enter into the necessary trust. It is difficult because we are locked into keeping in control. When we enter *hesychasm*, we are not in control. It is difficult because we are terrified of our own emptiness, and rather than be silent, we fill the empty space with empty chatter.

The closer we come to the reality of God, the more we come face-to-face with our own sinfulness. The gradual descent into our own wretchedness makes us realize that all our personae are illusory and false. This may lead to a renunciation of self, which has two parts: compunction and dread. Compunction is the acute understanding that our relationship with God is one between Creator and creature. It is the realization that we are insufficient and contingent upon his mercy. It liberates us from the illusion that our posturing is reality.

Dread, on the other hand, is nothingness, darkness, night, the painful epiphany that our relationship with God is one between the Almighty, Righteous, Holy One and a sinner who has repudiated him, and turned our back on who we truly are. The horror of dread is compounded with the realization that our infidelity is unrepentant and unrepentable. Our separation from God is due to a perverse attachment to self which is at the heart of what it means to be human. It leads to the moment of utter dereliction when we cry out with Jesus, "My God, my God, why hast thou forsaken me?"

This is not a once-and-for-all process. It remains part of the pattern of the Christian life. One of the great dangers of Christian living is to feel one has arrived, in piety if not in theology. If a genuine life of prayer is being entered into, God is continually re-creating us into the person he intends us to be. It is very easy to deceive ourselves and enter a comfortable existence. Once, after confessing a particularly troublesome sin, and telling my confessor that it felt like a gaping wound in my spirit, with great wisdom he told me he hoped the wound never healed. As long as it remained open and painful, I would remain united to Jesus Christ in his death, humbly repentant before God.

Three years ago I went on a retreat at St. Joseph's Trappist Abbey in Spencer, Massachusetts. One afternoon I was resting in my room reading Monica Furlong's biography of Thomas Merton. In it, Merton mentioned that if a person prayed the stations of the cross, when he or she got to the fourteenth station, God would answer the prayer. Well, I felt this was airy-fairy Roman Catholic piety, but since they had the stations around the guest house cloister, I decided I'd give it a try. I had a particularly self-indulgent prayer request to make.

To my surprise, I became deeply engrossed at each of the terra-cotta stations, touched by what Jesus had experienced in each moment. As I stood before the fourteenth station, I felt humiliated by my wanton selfishness. Still, it was worth a try, but as I offered my petty request, I became aware of the awesome holiness of the almighty God. It was like a weight that forced me down on my knees. In that moment all I wanted was to be faithful, to be obedient to him. In that moment, I understood John Donne's plea, "Batter my heart, three-personed God."

It is when we come to this moment of utter dereliction, this moment when we become united to Jesus in his death, this moment of casting ourselves on the mercy of the Father, that the Holy Spirit will lead us into a new life of inexpressible freedom. That is the moment of passing through death, Jesus' death, and entering into the Kingdom of God. Part of the passage is the realization that this intimacy with God is something that has already taken place in our baptism. It has already taken place in the heart of God. This *is* who we really are.

In the prayer of the heart, we come to identify more and more with the life of Jesus. We experience love, *agape*, a quality of love we have never experienced before. Agape is a thing of such value, we want to remain in this intimacy with the Lord. Agape brings us the understanding of four characteristics of God's love: it can be experienced only through grace; it is unmediated; only in it can we discover our true identity; and in it we enter perfect freedom. Jesus said, "I have come to set you free." In God's love we are set free from the power of sin, the need to draw everything into ourselves.

The result is a constant, loving, giving of ourselves to him, and a tremendous, deep, unshakable sense that we are beloved of God, that we belong to him. It was out of this experience Paul wrote in Romans 8,

> For I am sure that neither death, nor life, nor angels, nor principalities, nor things present, nor things to come, nor powers, nor height, nor depth, nor anything else in all creation, will be able to separate us from the love of God in Christ Jesus our Lord.

This is the peace that passes all understanding. Father William describes it as a peace, an apocalyptic peace, in the midst of life's joys and sorrows. "It gives us such an assurance," William told me, "that we as Christians can face any circumstance, no matter how horrible, with a genuine hope and joy."

The end of *hesychasm* is an awareness of our divine sonship or daughtership. We comprehend that God is living and working in us. Seeing both God's transcendence and immanence, we know who he really is. How one enters the prayer of the heart depends entirely on one's unique makeup, yet there are constants. It always takes place in an atmosphere of tranquility and solitude. It always takes place in uncomparable honesty. In it there is no hiding from ourselves or God. We see and acknowledge both the hideousness of our sin, and our belovedness by the Lord. There is a sense of loss of self. Yet in the mystery of the prayer, as we lose concern for self, we are given our true selves in Jesus Christ.

LIVING THE CHRISTIAN LIFE

Rather than causing a withdrawal from life, the prayer of the heart leads to realism and practicality, rooting us in the very reality of our lives. In the midst of the prayer, very often the Lord will lead me from focusing on him, to wrestle with the most mundane issues. He will move me from contemplating in wondrous joy of his awesome love to making me face the reality that I spoke harshly and unfairly that very morning to my son, David, or showing me how I had failed to fulfill a promise to visit a parishioner, or that I was late in paying a debt. I then know that I can't return to the prayer until I have made restitution. It is impossible to enter deeply into the love of God and not be given a greater love for others.

When I was in seminary, the most brilliant person in my class was named John Schneider. He was a historian by training, and once or twice when John explained some theory of history to me, I felt as if my mind had tripled in size. In reality, he'd just drawn me into his intelligence. When I went to Edinburgh University to work on my doctorate, John went to do the same at Cambridge University. Barbara and I visited with him and his wife, Winona, two or three times during our time in Britain. Once, after the four of us had toured Anglesly Abbey near Ely, we went on a stroll through the gardens. John and I moved off on our own and were discussing the history of revelation when he stopped suddenly, held my arm, and said, "Ken, I finally understand what God intends for us to do." Since it was John, I turned to him with total attention. He went on, "The most important thing God wants for us is to enjoy life."

Just as it is God's intention that we become, not Moses or the Apostle Paul, but simply ourselves, it is not God's intention for us to abandon our lives in order to adopt some heroic or saintly life-style. On the contrary, what he wants for us is to enter fully into the reality of our lives right now. There is no escapism in the life of prayer. God doesn't want to change our circumstances; he wants to redeem them. God doesn't want us to pray for the miraculous resolution of our problems. What he wants, and all he wants, is for us to be witnesses of redemption in the midst of our everyday existence.

Very shortly after my renewal in Christ, at the request of my boyhood minister, Norman Ream, I attended a day-long Transactional Analysis seminar at his church in Wauwatosa, Wisconsin. I had known many of the people in attendance since childhood. Some of them were friends of my parents, and I felt awkward entering their world as a peer. But I was fascinated by the presentation, and was able to give myself over to the event.

At one point the leader divided us into groups of about eight. He asked us to plan what we would do with the last day of our lives, if we knew in advance it was to be our last day, and there were no restrictions in terms of health or finances. We were then to share our thoughts with the small group. I love to let my imagination have free reign in circumstances like that, and in no time I was planning a day filled with excitement, achievement, and glory. I couldn't wait to tell everybody else.

The first person to speak was a woman in her early thirties. I hadn't met her before that day. As she spoke there was a simple purity in her voice. She wanted it to be a Saturday in the late spring. She would get up early, make herself a cup of coffee, and sit on the screened porch in the back of her house to watch the sun come up, listen to the birds sing, and open herself to the presence of God. Her three children would come down one by one and play together on the porch. She would prepare breakfast, and after her husband came down, they would eat together. Afterward, as the children played in the backyard, she and her husband would sit watching them, talking quietly as he read the morning paper and she knitted.

As she continued describing with such joy what was just a typical, ordinary day, the schemes of grandeur in my own imagination began to stink with rot. I have never forgotten her. Not only was she content with what God had given her, her greatest desires were fulfilled in the mundane events of her daily life. She didn't ask God to change her circumstances, because his redemption had already taken root in the ordinary, right where she already was. For me she embodied a person who understands and has entered the Kingdom of God here and now.

The life of prayer helps us to enter the reality of God's Kingdom here and now, and can redeem even the most loathsome circumstances. Probably more than anything else, I detest doing "youth work." To me it seems like glorified baby-sitting. You spend hours planning an event, getting the materials and supplies in order. You make sure all the kids know about it, and arrange transportation. In spite of that, you still have to pick up a dozen of them, drive them to the event, and take them home afterward. Everything I hate about youth work becomes heightened when the event is a weekend retreat. Then, on top of everything else, you have to cook for them, they keep you up all night with their games and tricks, and you're with them, constantly without break, for forty-eight straight hours!

When I was youth minister at St. Paul's Congregational Church in Claremont, California, our teenagers would go on retreats twice a year with about a dozen other church youth groups. The prospect was always so noisome, I would be on the verge of resigning my job in the preceding week. In the fall of 1975, we went to a camp up in the San Gabriel Mountains above Los Angeles. One Saturday after lunch, nearly all the kids were playing softball or hiking or finding some other way to injure themselves, and I had a couple of free hours.

It was a beautiful afternoon, with a gentle, warm breeze rustling through the oak trees. I was sitting at a sun-dappled picnic table chatting with a teenage boy who was from a church in Hollywood. I'd intended to go off to be by myself for a while, but it was so languidly pleasant, I tarried. The conversation drifted along, sometimes touching and circling around what it was like to be in the ministry, then moving on, to baseball, to the movies. Gradually, imperceptibly, as we sat in that leaf-filtered sunlight, I felt that God himself was with us, perfecting the moment. We didn't go anywhere. He came to us. Heaven came down and touched that picnic site. Through God's grace, we entered the Kingdom.

God is not in the business of changing our circumstances; he's in the business of redeeming them. The life of prayer, particularly a life devoted to the prayer of the heart, will lead to a sacrificial love for others. In union with Christ, as we experience at the same time our utter dereliction and the understanding that we are loved and cherished by God, he enables us to see our solidarity with others. He transforms our selfishness and fear into sympathy and compassion. Every detail of our lives is drawn into the prayer, and we begin to see God's presence in every moment, and in every person. He enables us to reach out in love to those in need, not for our own benefit, not even for them, but for him.

When Father William Wilson left New Melleray Abbey in the fall of 1981, called by God to make a pilgrimage among the poor, circumstances led him to the Maryknoll Language Institute in Cochabomba, Bolivia. He went there for six months to learn Spanish, and prayed that the Lord would show him how, as a contemplative, he was to make a redemptive witness among the poor. He was living in Cochabomba's barrio, and although alone, he kept up his Trappist discipline of prayer. As he became involved in the lives of his neighbors, and helped them to deal with some of their problems, he slowly understood that he didn't have to go anywhere. He was already living and witnessing among the poor.

He met an Austrian priest who served several villages of the Quechua Indians in the high Andes, far from civilization. In the summer of 1982 this priest invited William to take up residence as a monk in the Quechua village of Aramasi. He went to Aramasi that summer and established a contemplative presence there.

The Quechua are among the poorest people in the world. They live on a diet of potatoes, corn, some wheat, an occasional egg, and a little goat milk. Their small patches of soil claimed from the mountain slopes are plowed with sharpened sticks. Because of the lack of protein in their diet, the children's brains don't develop fully, so they have become an entire race with subhuman intelligence. They drink the same water that they relieve themselves in, so they are parasite-ridden as well as malnourished. For the average Quechua in the high Andes, life is brutal and short.

William says that the Quechua are baptized, but unevangelized. Their faith in Jesus Christ is murkily confused with animism. Their own Indian culture is slowly dying, yet they have not yet been absorbed into the dominant Spanish culture. The Quechua are no longer economically self-sufficient, but need to earn Bolivian pesos in order to buy clothes and other necessities.

William began a life of prayer and witness among these Indians in 1982. At that time he was joined by Columbia Guare, who had been abbess of the Trappistine Our Lady of the Mississippi Convent, in Dubuque, Iowa. Through funds raised in the United States, they built a retreat house in Cochabomba, and began a monastic community in Aramasi with hermitages and guest quarters. In Aramasi, they built a modern clinic which they have staffed with a doctor and nurse, who direct a nutritional program for the children. They have also helped with reconstruction of the village school, and supplement the teachers' salaries.

In June of 1986, I visited William and Columba in Bolivia. The road from Cochabomba to Aramasi has to be one of the worst in all creation. Narrow, strewn with fallen rocks, rutted, crossing over river beds, as it climbs high into the Andes it twists perilously around sharp turns with enormous cliffs falling immediately off the edge of the road. Yet the Aramasi Valley, above ten thousand feet, is starkly beautiful, with eucalyptus trees clustered along the river bank and high peaks layered to the horizon.

The tiny monastic community lives an austere life, following a modified form of the Benedictine Rule. There is no electricity or running water. They get up in the dark at four in the morning and gather in the stark parish church for *matins*. Following the Psalms, candles are blown out, and they have a silent prayer vigil for an hour and forty-five minutes. As dawn breaks, and light begins to filter into the dark church, they have *lauds*, usually with a discussion on the passages from Scripture appointed for the day. After a brief break, they gather again for the celebration of the Eucharist. A simple breakfast of bread and cheese, with maybe an egg, follows. The day is spent among the Indians, helping in the clinic or school, or simply responding to the problems that are brought to them. They gather for another meal in the midafternoon, and after some time for reading or meditating, they go back to the church for *vespers* followed by *compline*. They are in their hermitages for the night at about eight o'clock.

When I visited, I entered their discipline with some difficulty. The first morning, the vigil of silence in the frigid darkness was an interminable agony. But each morning I became more comfortable, and after several days I was eager to enter the prayer. When I accompanied William on his rounds through the village, I encountered another kind of difficulty. Washing is not part of the Quechua culture. Some of the people I met were covered with fifty years of grime. The smell, which I found barely tolerable, has something of the musky quality of the lair of a wild animal.

One morning I met the village elders. William wanted to take my picture with the head man, whose name is Juan Salazar. As we stood together, Don Juan put his arm around my shoulder. The smile on my face was frozen as I wondered how many millions of microbes were crawling off him onto my body. At the Sunday morning mass, William asked me to bless the thirty or so children who were present. Moving my hand from head to head, blessing them in the name of the Father, Son, and Holy Spirit, I had to fight a desire to run off and scrub my hand. William and Columba are in Aramasi to love and serve God and the

Quechua. I found the Indians to be so physically repulsive, my times of prayer were dominated by the question, "How, Lord, can I possibly love these people?"

Among the almost unbelievable poverty of the Quechua of Aramasi, the poorest family was that of a widow named Delicia. She is a person of wonderful dignity. When I was there, William took her six candles. Later that same day she came and gave him one egg. She had a little boy named Luciano, who had had an ear infection for over a year. The nurse in the clinic had been unable to cure it with antibiotics. It was draining blood and pus, and the nurse was afraid he would go deaf, or if the infection entered the bone, he would die. William decided that when he took me into Cochabomba to return to New York, he would also take Luciano to a hospital there.

I'd seen Luciano once or twice before, and he looked like all the other boys, dressed in filthy rags. Yet when we were ready to leave, he was standing next to the jeep, wearing a new bright green plaid sweater. He was relatively clean, and had a handkerchief neatly folded in his pocket. A small wrapped bundle of food was slung from his shoulder. The Quechua are not affectionate people, and his mother didn't even wave good-bye as we left the village. He sat next to me in the backseat, on the long two-hour drive over the twisting mountain road. Luciano was stiff with fright because he had never before left Aramasi.

Once we entered the city, the traffic, crowds, and swirl of colors and sights made him even more rigid. He mechanically followed as we went to the doctor, who took a culture and said the infection would be easy to cure once properly diagnosed. When William stopped for an errand, I bought Luciano an ice cream bar. It was the first time he had ever eaten ice cream. As he munched away, a little wisp of a smile flickered around the corners of his mouth.

I was dropped off in the city to see a work project at a school that William was sponsoring. William drove off to his retreat house with the little boy. When I arrived at the house an hour later, Luciano was standing behind the gate, clinging to its bars. He was the most forlorn person I'd ever seen. I suddenly knew. In that moment, I knew how he felt. I went in and picked him up. He clung fiercely to my neck. Mother Columba found a bottle of soap bubbles with a wand to blow them. I spent an hour teaching Luciano how to blow bubbles. That night, after dark, I held him up so he could look over the wall to see the sparkling lights of the city, stretching for miles all across the valley below.

The next morning when I got up, Luciano had already been up for over an hour, blowing bubbles in the courtyard. He had learned how to blow a string of small bubbles. He also had learned how to blow one big bubble, capture it on the end of the wand, and burst it on his nose as he laughed gleefully. I taught him to do a "high five" with every string of bubbles. And every time he burst a big bubble on his nose, I taught him to say his first word in English, "Okay!" God had shown me how easy it is to love and serve a boy like Luciano.

Father William lives a life of prayer in the high Andes of Bolivia. He doesn't know what the future will bring. In Aramasi, there are so many germs in the food, air, and water that he is under constant assault. His intestines are riddled with parasites, and he's had a kidney infection for months. He doesn't know what the future will bring, but he knows that the future is Jesus. Quoting Job, he recently said to me, "Even though he kill me, I will trust in him."

THE END OF PRAYER

God calls every human being to a life of prayer. Not William's, not mine, but his or her own life of prayer. We pray, not to get what we want, but in order to enter into intimacy with God. In that intimacy, in union with Jesus Christ, we discover our true identity as beloved children of God. In this prayer we are drawn into the life of the Trinity. We know the fullness of the love, joy, and peace of God himself.

The life of prayer developed by any individual will be uniquely his or her own, because ultimately it is about his or her unique relationship with God. No one else in the universe can know God the way you can, because no one else in the universe is you. Although the discipline of prayer may manifest itself in a variety of ways, it will have constants shared with every other Christian. It will lead to the realization that intimacy with God is of incomparable value. All else pales next to it. It will lead to fellowship, *koinonia*, with other Christians. It will lead to loving, and perhaps self-sacrificing, service for those in need. It will lead to deep involvement with life, not in order to flee from or change our circumstances, but to redeem them for God.

In prayer, the power of the Holy Spirit transforms us. In the power of the Holy Spirit we become people who no longer yearn for the past, and no longer dream of power and glory in the future. No, because God intends us to be people who live in the present, with joy. In prayer, we are transformed by God to be people who no longer live for self but for others. Through faith in Jesus Christ and a discipline of prayer we enter a new quality of existence. The love, peace, and joy of God become ours. We are the future.

SELECTED BIBLIOGRAPHY

Athanasius. *The Life of Anthony and the Letter to Marcellinus*. New York: Paulist Press, 1980.

Augustine of Hippo. *Selected Writings*. New York: Paulist Press, 1984.

Bernard of Clairvaux. *On the Song of Songs*. 4 vols. Kalamazoo, Mich.: Cistercian Publications, 1986.

Bonaventure. *The Life of St. Francis*. Translated by Ewart Cousins. New York: Paulist Press, 1978.

Bonhoeffer, Dietrich. *The Cost of Discipleship*. Translated by R. H. Fuller. New York: Macmillan, 1967.

———. *Life Together*. Translated by John Doberstein. New York: Harper & Row, 1954.

The Book of Common Prayer. New York: The Church Hymnal Corporation, 1978.

Caretto, Carlo. *Letters From the Desert*. Translated by Rose Mary Hancock. Maryknoll, N.Y.: Orbis Books, 1972.

The Cloud of Unknowing. Garden City, N.Y.: Image Books, 1973.

Denney, James. *Studies in Theology*, Grand Rapids, Mich.: Baker, 1976.

Eckhardt, Meister. *Essential Sermons, Commentaries, Treatises, and Defense*. Translated by Edmund Colledge and Bernard McGinn. New York: Paulist Press, 1981.

Foster, Richard J. *Celebration of Discipline*. San Francisco: Harper & Row, 1978.

Francis and Clare. *The Complete Works*. Translated by Regis J. Armstrong and Ignatius C. Brady. New York: Paulist Press, 1982.

Francis de Sales. *Introduction to the Devout Life*. Translated by John K. Ryan. New York: Harper & Row, 1949.

Holmes, Urban T. *A History of Christian Spirituality*. New York: Seabury Press, 1980.

Ignatius of Loyola. *The Spiritual Exercises*. Translated by David J. Fleming. St. Louis: Institute of Jesuit Sources, 1978.

John of the Cross. *The Ascent of Mount Carmel*. Translated by E. Allison Peers. Garden City, N.Y.: Doubleday, 1958.

———. *The Dark Night of the Soul*. Translated by E. Allison Peers. Garden City, N.Y.: Doubleday, 1959.

Julian of Norwich. *Revelations of Divine Love*. New York: Penguin Books, 1966.

Kelsey, Morton. *Companions on the Inner Way*. New York: Crossroad, 1984.

Kempis, Thomas à. *The Imitation of Christ*. Translated

by Harold Gardiner. Garden City, N.Y.: Double-day, 1955.

Law, William. *A Serious Call to a Devout and Holy Life*. New York: Paulist Press, 1978.

Lawrence of the Resurrection, Brother. *The Practice of the Presence of God*. New York: Doubleday, 1977.

Leech, Kenneth. *Soul Friend*. San Francisco: Harper & Row, 1977.

———. *True Prayer: An Invitation to Christian Spirituality*. San Francisco: Harper & Row, 1980.

Lewis, C. S. *Mere Christianity*. New York: Macmillan, 1964.

———. *The Problem of Pain*. New York: Macmillan, 1964.

Linn, Mathew and Dennis. *Healing Life's Hurts*. New York: Paulist Press, 1978.

Luther, Martin. *Letters of Spiritual Counsel*. Philadelphia: Westminster Press, 1955.

Marty, Martin E. *A Cry of Absence*. San Francisco: Harper & Row, 1983.

McNutt, Francis. *Healing*. New York: Bantam Books, 1974.

Merton, Thomas. *Contemplative Prayer*. Garden City, N.Y.: Image Books, 1971.

———. *The New Man*. New York: Farrar, Straus & Giroux, 1961.

———. *New Seeds of Contemplation*. New York: New Directions, 1961.

Nouwen, Henri. *The Way of the Heart*. New York: Seabury Press, 1981.

————. *The Wounded Healer*. Garden City, N.Y.: Image Books, 1979.

O'Connor, Elizabeth. *Call to Commitment*. San Francisco: Harper & Row, 1963.

Pascal, Blaise. *Pensées*. Translated by A. J. Krailsheimer. New York: Penguin Books, 1966.

Pennington, M. Basil. *Centering Prayer*. Garden City, N.Y.: Doubleday, 1982.

Price, Charles P., and Louis Weil. *Liturgy for Living*. New York: Seabury Press, 1979.

Quaker Spirituality. New York: Paulist Press, 1984.

Teresa of Avila. *The Interior Castle*. Translated by E. Allison Peers. Garden City, N.Y.: Doubleday, 1961.

Thornton, Martin. *English Spirituality*. Cambridge, Mass.: Cowley, 1983.

————. *Spiritual Direction*. Cambridge, Mass.: Cowley, 1984.

Underhill, Evelyn. *Mysticism*. New York: Dutton, 1961.

Ward, Bendicta. *The Sayings of the Desert Fathers*. London: Mowbray, 1975.

The Way of the Pilgrim. Translated by R. M. French. New York: Harper & Brothers, 1952.

Weil, Simone. *The Simone Weil Reader*. New York: McKay, 1977.

Wesley, John and Charles. *Selected Writings and Hymns*. New York: Paulist Press, 1981.

INDEX

233

ABOUT THE AUTHOR

Descended from a long line of clerics, Kenneth Swanson was born in Minnesota and raised in Wisconsin. He has earned degrees from the University of Wisconsin, Fuller Theological Seminary, and Edinburgh University. An Episcopal priest, Dr. Swanson has served parishes in California, Scotland, and New York. Although his academic specialty is Hinduism in the West, as a parish priest he has focused on developing an extensive ministry in spiritual direction. Dr. Swanson, his wife Barbara, and their two children, David and Katrina, spend their happiest hours at their home in the Catskills. From this mountain retreat, he and his son make regular forays to Queens and the Bronx to indulge in their great passion: baseball.